FRESH WOODS
PASTURES NEW

Ian Niall

Illustrated by
Barbara Greg

LITTLE TOLLER BOOKS
an imprint of THE DOVECOTE PRESS

This paperback edition published in 2012 by
Little Toller Books
Stanbridge, Wimborne Minster, Dorset BH21 4JD
Fresh Woods first published in 1951 by William Heinemann
Pastures New first published in 1952 by William Heinemann

ISBN 978-1-908213-08-2

Text © The Estate of Ian Niall 2012
Engravings © The Estate of Barbara Greg 2012
Introduction © Andrew McNeillie 2012

We have made every reasonable effort to trace the executors of
Barbara Greg's estate, and would welcome any further information

Typeset in Monotype Sabon by Little Toller Books
Printed in Spain by GraphyCems, Navarra

All papers used by Little Toller Books and the Dovecote Press
are natural, recyclable products made from
wood grown in sustainable, well-managed forests

A CIP catalogue record for this book is available
from the British Library

1 3 5 7 9 8 6 4 2

INTRODUCTION

Andrew McNeillie

T HE TWO COMPANION BOOKS published together for the first time here
are effectively sequels to Ian Niall's much-loved classic *The Poacher's
Handbook* (1950). *Fresh Woods* appeared in 1951, *Pastures New* a year
later. All three haunt the same territory and all three are haunted in
turn by Barbara Greg's beautifully judged grainy woodcuts, which are
miraculously at one with the tenor of the texts they illustrate. The books
were originally produced by Heinemann to resemble each other, and so
made an informal trilogy with *The Poacher's Handbook*. That work has
never been out of print in more than sixty years. But the two volumes
issued here have been unavailable for decades. So it is heartening and a
great service to Ian Niall's many admirers, and to readers yet to discover
him, to have them published again at last. As contemporary reviewers
regularly noted, Niall was 'a born writer' and the author of 'remarkable
English prose'. The remarkable nature of that prose is nowhere more
evident than in the works that follow in this book.

I hope readers will not mind being reminded that the titles of these
twin works derive from Milton's elegy 'Lycidas':

> And now the sun had stretched out all the hills,
> And now was dropped into the western bay;
> At last he rose, and twitched his mantle blue:
> Tomorrow to fresh woods, and pastures new.

And indeed it can be said they differ from *The Poacher's Handbook*,
their only begetter, in being more avowedly elegiac. I believe they are also
more extraordinary in the way they sustain their lyrical improvisation
and manage their transitions. Book-length essays without chapter breaks,

they lack the kind of structural underpinning an account of poaching and its various methods more readily provides. Poaching remains a sporadic theme, as does shooting. In this respect these books describe a world nearer to that of the nineteenth-century's Richard Jefferies than to the present day. But primarily they are about observation and a vigorous passion for the natural world, the life of woodland and field, as first seen through the eyes of a solitary child. They have a timeless quality in their particular articulation of memory, one found more commonly in poetry. In which respect not Milton but Wordsworth springs first to mind. These works are preludes without epic aspiration.

Ian Niall was the pen name of John McNeillie. He was born in 1916, at Old Kilpatrick near Dalmuir on the banks of the Firth of Clyde. But he spent the formative part of his early childhood in the care of his paternal grandparents, tenants at North Clutag Farm in the Machars of Wigtownshire, a far-flung south-westerly corner of Scotland. This idyllic time, as he would come to see it, was the ground of the greater part of his non-fictional writing, including and beyond *Fresh Woods* and *Pastures New*. Subsequent school holidays spent exclusively at his grandparents' farm would consolidate these early impressions and enrich them with wider adventures farther afield in the district. He lived to observe not just the countryside but its inhabitants, and its migrant populations too, as work or the hope of work brought them up the farm lane. Niall's love of nature included human nature, above all in its commonality. He was a solitary but no misanthrope, as many nature writers have been accused of being, and not always without reason.

By the early 1950s Niall enjoyed the kind of critical approval most authors can only ever dream might one day come their way. *The Poacher's Handbook* undoubtedly played a major part in establishing his name as a ruralist, in the great tradition of Jefferies, whose numerous classics include *The Amateur Poacher* (1879). In December 1953 Niall would begin what would become a forty-plus-year stint as the author of a *Country Life* weekly column, 'A Countryman's Notes', never missing a week. An extract from *The Poacher's Handbook* had appeared in that journal's pages in August 1950, and he'd contributed a few pieces there in the interim, including in January 1953, from *Pastures New*, 'The Old Farm Gun' accompanied by a Barbara Greg woodcut.

Not that Ian Niall hadn't made headlines before. In 1948 Heinemann published his novel *No Resting Place*, a story of traveller people in the exact terrain of the rural trilogy. This book was filmed in County Wicklow by the documentarist Paul Rotha with Michael Gough in the leading role supported by Abbey and Gate Theatre players. The film represented Britain at the Venice Film Festival and the book itself sold just short of 10,000 copies in its first six months. Even before this its author had found fame (and notoriety) with a precocious debut. He was twenty-two when Putnam of London and New York published John McNeillie's first book *Wigtown Ploughman: Part of his Life* (1939). This was a radical Zolaesque novel critical of the living and working conditions of the labouring poor of the Machars of Wigtownshire. Serialised in the *Glasgow Sunday Mail*, it caused a furore that at one point reached as far as the House of Commons. Ian Niall would later disown this work, as crudely executed. But the germ of his rural lyricism is strongly marked in its pages, as it is in *No Resting Place*, the success of which he never quite recaptured, though he repeatedly tried to do so.

John McNeillie's fortunes were derailed by the outbreak of the Second World War, as were those of so many. The catastrophe brought him to Old Colwyn on the North Wales coast, to work in a precision-tool engineering factory for the duration, and as it proved long after. Here, beside the Irish Sea, directly due south from the Machars of Wigtownshire, was born Ian Niall. And here a great number of his books were written, including *Fresh Woods* and *Pastures New*, as at moments their pages reveal.

We say absence makes the heart grow fonder. But we should add that it cannot do so without presence. In the pages you are about to read the gap between the two is opened and closed with graceful timing, in a syntax of the simplest and most limpid order. There is no harder way to write and Niall was aware of this. Perhaps if there is a key to his approach it's the one he provides himself in the first pages of *Fresh Woods*: 'when a thing brings happiness it is not my way to analyse myself into clinical indifference, discovering the simple cause of my delight and, perhaps thereby destroying it.' His way is to tell you what he has seen in wonder and done with excited pleasure, and to reflect on these in terms of mutability and ongoing human endeavour in the countryside. He is not afraid of sentiment or nostalgia but his heart's firmly shut to sentimentality.

The only pauses in Niall's narrative resemble those we make in conversation, as if to take breath, as one strand of a story runs its course to lead all but at once to another, and so on, seamlessly compelled. The voice in these books is full of invention and also of collusion or inclusion. Those who have read *The Poacher's Handbook* will at once recognise the seductive mode: 'Come with me to the low planting as it was when I was small . . .' *Fresh Woods* treads woods in Scotland and in Wales. *Pastures New* walks the ground of North Clutag Farm more exclusively.

Niall's parents gave him a typewriter when he was twenty-one. The first nineteen chapters of his first book (begun when he was nineteen) were handwritten. Thereafter he typed and the sentences spilled from his head word-for-word as you read them. He rarely rewrote and barely revised. His thought bodied forth onto the page just like speech meeting the air. He had tremendous facility. Yet he would confess to Barbara Greg in a letter of 28 May 1951 that '*Fresh Woods* put a great strain on me'.

It is unusual in his archive to find anything handwritten and anything approaching rehearsal. But, uniquely, while in Wicklow during the filming of *No Resting Place* he made the following entry in a little paperbound notebook:

This book, a companion to *Fresh Woods*, is the story of fields. I make no excuse for taking my readers into the fields of my boyhood, the home paddocks and the back hills where the blackface sheep grazed the fields where I searched for the nest of the peewit and barefooted and light-hearted, chased the wild bees with a bottle containing sugar and clover heads, hoping to capture them and have their furry beauty forever in my possession. I wandered the fields of this story to find a toad, to put to flight a covey of partridges and smell the myrtle at the edge of the bog. The horizon of the less fortunate townsman is in the lines, the cubes, the rectangles and triangles of buildings and roofs. My horizon has really always been the round hills my father's family farmed. Even when I was away from them, this horizon was mine. It is to New Pastures I ask you to come, in the fresh air of morning as it was when I was a child.

Beyond this we are also fortunate in the survival of correspondence with Barbara Greg (1900-1983). She had studied at the Slade School, a pupil of one of the great masters of reproductive wood engraving, W.T. Smith. With her future husband, Norman Janes, she taught wood engraving at the Slade for a period from 1938. As the reader might guess, Greg took much inspiration from Thomas Bewick's example.

That she collaborated closely with her author emerges from their letters. They had consulted much over *The Poacher's Handbook*: 'The hare's tail – could it be shortened and the snare's noose tightened? . . . I think the pheasant wings should be a little longer . . . The partridge's tail should be shorter . . .' 'Please forget about the pheasant's wings. I had no idea what my suggestions might involve'. 'I shall always be indebted to you for making the *Handbook* the success it is', he wrote to her on 27 December 1950. Much later in life he would lament not having worked with her again and described her as technically the equal of the bolder Tunnicliffe.

For some time, through November 1949 and February 1950, Niall refers in his letters to a new book with the title 'Rain on the Skylight', being 'reminiscences of a Scottish farm and boyhood'. He was half way through writing it, he told Greg on 12 February. By 22 April the book he is writing is called 'Fresh Woods' and this seems to be not necessarily entirely the same with 'Rain on the Skylight', of which no typescript and no mention beyond the correspondence has been found. Given Niall's businesslike approach to his work it is probable that he simply discarded the earlier foray and began afresh. Nothing daunted, it seemed: he would hammer away at his typewriter in the little alcove of our living room, under the hot-water tank cupboard, between the fireplace and the window next to our Welsh backyard, regardless of domestic din about him, in a reverie, dreaming of 'a time long ago' . . . as when

> I had a sudden fancy to taste plover eggs again, I wrote to a cousin who farmed in the north and he made a Sunday walk and gathered me a dozen. The box came by post. I scrambled to cut the string, but, alas, the eggs were broken. I could only stand with the fragments of shell in my hands and remember the days of my childhood when I walked those same acres in search of the peewit's nest. I was downcast and yet there was a certain nostalgic pleasure in receiving the package. I looked at it again. It was tied with binder twine, a hastily made parcel, something from the far moss. The cry of the birds sounded in my ears as I looked at it.

With which missed opportunity, I'm pleased to have served you a taster of what follows.

Andrew McNeillie
Thame, 2012

FRESH WOODS

THE WOODS OF MY STORY are, or were, in Scotland and in Wales. Some of them have fallen to the sawmill and the lumberman and have memorials of mountains of sawdust on which nothing will grow, but some are still there, those old woods of gnarled Welsh oak, those thickets of hazel, blackthorn and elder, spindle-tangled, draped with ivy, honeysuckle and creeper. Here and there, even now, I can see them, spruce fringing a hill on the skyline, ash, elm and chestnut in a hollow, making shelter for the wintering woodcock, the migrant pigeon from Scandinavia. In this one, on the bleak slope above the lake, I stood half a day watching the coming and going of pigeons, crows, magpies and the little owl.

The wood in the hollow had hardly encompassed me before I heard the derisive laughter of the yaffle as he left, darting and undulating across the field, the greenest of green feathers, the reddest of red above his pickaxe beak. All of them sheltered me on grey winter days and shaded me in summer while I fought the midges and the flies. In the wood that contained the green-scummed pool I gathered crab apples and was stung in the eye by a wasp that had been uprooted from its nest by a foraging badger. In the little fir plantation I fell asleep with an old hammer gun cradled in my arms, and the gun, hair-triggered and unsafe, blew a great branch from the tree above my head and brought me to frightened life, feeling myself and wondering for an instant whether I was in this world or the next. In half a dozen woods my heart beat fast and I watched the keeper pass.

I was not always there to listen to the song of the wren, to watch the little spotted woodpecker, no bigger than the nuthatch. I was not always there to poach, although I have done my share. I suppose often enough I could not have told you why I was there, unless to be soothed by the whisper of the leaves, the hushing of the pine tops. Ask a man why he dallies by the water or why he seeks a mountain top. Ask a man why he lives if not to stand in contemplation at times. I have no excuse to offer other than that which the reader will find between the covers of this book, the story of my idle days, and if we linger a while on a foxglove-spattered slope that was once a wood, it is only while I bring the wood back again, perhaps to shoot that full-cropped pigeon coming in, perhaps only to study the tree and its crop of cones, or the trapezean leaps of the squirrel.

My small son and daughter like nothing better than to be taken to the woods behind the village. It is true the woods have gone farther back and the timber-hungry world has had its way with what once were leafy glades, sun-dappled, hollow-echoed. The woods have a fascination for the young. It may be that some primeval instinct operates. I can recall that the woods beckoned when I was no more than a toddler. That they have continued to do so may mean that I have much of the daydreamer in my make-up, but when a thing brings happiness it is not my way to analyse myself into clinical indifference, discovering the simple cause of my delight and, perhaps thereby destroying it.

Come with me to the low planting as it was when I was small. It stands at the foot of the hill, bounded on one side by the moss, with gorse grown so tall that bullocks are lost there, let alone the blackface sheep. The moss gives something to the little planting, a flanking of round rushes, peat banks where the curlew, the peewit and the nightjar nest. The black rabbit lives here, feeding out on the springy fine grass, lifting himself on his back legs and cocking his ears, bolting back to safety in the planting through a hole in the drystone wall. The black rabbit – there is always one – is not so much black as sooty brown, rich brown like the fur of nothing else. He is always obvious because he bobs in the midst of a scampering of grey rabbits, each with its own entry to the planting, through rush tunnels and holes, or over a low spot on the wall. The ground is alive with their flight, and all at once you have it to yourself, the gorse mounds, the cotton grass, the call of the bird across the moss. I

have never considered the black rabbit and why he is so; perhaps he is a
freak of inbreeding, pigment or selection, or perhaps it is simply that he
is the only one of that alert, speeding crowd that could remain out there,
a blend with the peat bank. How often have I seen him, the old moss
rabbit, so beautiful. His flesh was always said to be whiter than that of
his grey brothers, but I cannot remember ever having eaten one.

All my life I have felt a happiness when looking towards the west. It
may have something to do with the fact that the light is always freshest
and brightest on the western sky. The sun may rise and fill the east with
reds and gold, but what loveliness there is when one looks with the light,
seeing it touch the tops of sleeping trees, brightening the last clouds of
night.

The little planting is to the west of the farm, huddled in the shelter of
the hill, it holds its shadows longer. Its trees have mist and enchantment
when day is riding in the east. There is a blueness among the firs and the
pigeons seem to vanish into its depths, enveloping and safe. Up the hollow,
along the bracken-bordered ditch, close to the high march wall, the little
planting is an invitation to adventure. When we are within reach of this
wonderland, to see the ferns on one of its knolls, the hawthorn barrier
on two sides, we hear the magpie shaking his pillbox in its caverns, the
endless, hoarse love-talk of the doves. It is a forbidden place. Indeed, it
is well fenced against trespassers. The drystone wall is old, and built, as

are all the walls in this district, with rounded, glacier-rolled rocks. These stones, or boulders, are moss-grown and very, very wobbly. Touch one and a dozen crash down, and they are large stones, capable of breaking a man's leg, or flattening his boot. The hedge of thorn is impenetrable. The wall is reinforced by an ancient barbed wire fence.

We stand in the corner of the march dike, for a drystone wall is never anything but that good old Scots thing, a dike, a dike of grey-lichened stones where the boundary is open, or green-mossed boulders where a wood gives shelter. In this corner, shaded by an alder, a storm-forced fir leaning drunkenly, and the arms of an ash, we stand and peel the heavy skin of moss from the stones and listen. Away in the depths – how much bigger a wood is when one is young – across the marshy ground, up on the hillock, the little knowe, a cock pheasant crows or a small bird twitters. The bracken and ferns sway, a sort of sigh breathes through the trees, bringing a hundred alluring scents, scents of mouldering leaves, of myrtle, of pine resin, pollen of a late-blossoming tree. Others may look at the mountain, at its majesty, its cloud shadows racing, or at the smooth, heavy flow of the river, but we stand at the march wall, determined to go into the wood. We must gather confidence. It is not that we are afraid of the brooding trees, of being alone on that soundproofed carpet of pine needles and leaves. We are used to being alone, used to the shadows, happy in the attic bedroom without an oil lamp when the family are busy at the milking, grooming horses, locking up fowls, feeding sows and wandering the court with swinging storm lanterns. The little planting is the keeper's domain. We have to be sure that he is not about. We have to be sure that we can cross the wall and the fence without mishap and come out again. We have to be sure, too, that no one at home sees us, for everyone there seems to be scanning the fields when we venture to the stream to fish, wade in the march gate pool to put up the snipe or try ourselves as stalkers of grouse feeding on the corn stooks.

Hardly have we clambered the dike, ducked the wire, than the world of the little planting has word of us. A pigeon bursts out of a fir above our heads and beats off over the roof of the wood, gathering another

and another. How simple is their escape. The burst of speed takes them
round the edge of the wood, up, up, and they are swinging away, across
the hill, over the turnips, the harvest field, the grazing sheep. A crumbling
of twig drops from the tree, a feather gently tumbles down and comes
to rest on the carpet of the wood, as silently as a duck's feather kissing
the water. Pick up this fragment, this thing of delicate beauty, the feather
of the ring dove, plump-breasted, blue tail tipped with black, rose-
tinged breast and neck with its metallic sheen below the white ring.
Had he stayed, had you had him in your hand, you might have seen the
wonderful grey and red marking on his feet, the active movement of his
head, but he is gone. He belongs to the countryside, to this wood and the
far wood, to the oatfield and the thorn tree. Up there he left a mate and
a nest. We stand and stare with the feather in our fingers. The hen rears
on the nest, watching us through that thick screen of spruce. Her heart
beats fast, some little thing makes it all unbearable and she, too, bursts
into the late summer sky, leaving the nest, this third or fourth brood, this
unhatched egg and bald, ugly chick. She does not fly so far, but sweeps

in at the pine top at the far corner, alighting nervously, moving along the branch, listening, watching, ready to go again, but not too far, back in a climb and a glide to some fresh vantage point, where she can wait until the drum of the wood stops sounding with our clumsy progress.

There is a little hill in the low planting, a hill that is itself a forest, a forest of bracken as tall as a man: bend low and you see the world of the rabbit, the stoat, the pheasant. You see the fallen tree and the tangle of its broken branches. There is a stench about this place, an unbearable odour. Perhaps some animal has died, perhaps some wounded bird has glided in and fallen to die in the forest of the bracken? No, here the stinkhorn grows, that strange horn-shaped fungus that repels everything but its complement of flies. The rain that has soaked the earth has grown fungus, others that are beautiful grow on the mouldering tree, oak-hued, tough, pink-tinted, finger-staining. It is strange, but to most countrymen all of these funguses are poisonous. I suppose it is a question of having a simple rule, touch none and you cannot die by them, the rule that so many people apply to snakes. Every snake is an adder, beware them all, yet on this very hill, higher, where the trees open a little to the sky and a few stones lie about, a great fat snake rests on its coils, the grass snake, taking the last of summer's warmth before going back to its hole beneath the tree. This one so heavy, so wicked-looking and so harmless, is the female that laid her eggs in the warm mould. Turn them with your foot, these linked cells, and you will see where the young emerged, one, two, ten, twenty, how many? Perhaps, like the man with the seeds, there was one for the crow and one to grow, or the world would soon be filled with the grass snake family. The snake feels the movement in the ground and turns. The thin grass hisses and makes you shiver, and the snake hurries away across the floor of the wood to some hideout, dark and damp.

Now we are at the summit of the hill, looking at the rowan tree, bowed with its great crop of berries. Nothing in the wood is so red as the berries of the rowan, nothing so beautiful as the red and the green above the bracken. Every tree seems to have its own little island of space where no bracken grows, except those great pines. Look up into the tops

of the pines and you see that broken bark, ruddy and sun-kissed, those swaying arms of the trees looking black against the sky. These are the tallest trees in the wood, dwarfing the ash, the elm, the sycamore. Here, when the pigeons come back, they will take their first pause, bobbing on the top to look over the wood and then going down, spreading their wings and sailing to the firs. Stand a long time here and you will hear them come back, that fluttering in to perch, that movement from one tree to another. This is the time the wood pigeon lives for, when his crop is filled with ripe grain, when the sun is in the high trees and he can hear the love-talk carried on the wind from other, faraway woods. Watch him take that short flight from the sheer joy of being alive, listen to him clap his wings and then sail along the trees, see the light through his wings as he does it and know that, whoever has him in a pie in November, he had his summer above the firs when all the countryside was alive with harvest activity. He had his summer and his spring when the young peas were sprouting, filling his crop until he must surely have felt heavy, carrying that load of forty or fifty sprouted seeds across the harrowed fields.

Behind the rowan tree stands the thickest part of the little planting where the firs crowd like soldiers on parade, so close, so crowded that they die as they all grow together towards the sky, leaving nothing below their top branches but a mass of dead twigs in which the spider makes his web. This strange way of planting trees was not devised by a man who loved a wood or a tree, but by someone who wanted to make cover for game, someone who did not care if the trees strangled each other, so long as a long-tailed bird could be scared out by the beaters. It is possible to get through this barrier by crawling on hands and knees. Like the forest of bracken, this untrodden ground beneath the firs belongs to the rabbit and the ground bird, the pheasant that steers its way through the wood, more aware of our coming than any other bird, as conscious of the vibration in the air as the snake is of the vibration in the ground. Crawling through this barrier we disturb a second nesting pigeon and an owl deserts his perch and goes off into the gloom of another thicket, flying silently, low, perching in at the side of a tree trunk and becoming at once motionless and invisible. The wren sings somewhere on the side of the moss, a pigeon sweeps over and turns back. We are at the thorn tree hedge, stumbling over the hidden rabbit holes, fending off the trailing arm of a blackberry tangle.

It is quiet now. The wood seems to hold its breath and then the pigeon begins his love-talk. Soon another speaks. The little wood is alive. At once the owl throws himself off his perch – there was too much light where he sat – and goes back to his old roost on the limed spar. A squirrel runs up the trunk of a tree and plays hide and seek with us, now disappearing, scuttling up a limb out of our sight, peering at us from a height that would make us dizzy, throwing himself on to the very tip of the branch of a neighbouring pine. Again the wren sings and the magpie scolds, flirting his tail and chasing his brothers across the wood.

At home the dog is barking the cows in for milking. It is time we went back to tea. The scones are hot, the butter is fresh from the cool milkhouse, the cream is thick and rich. Brush the twigs from your hair, the moss from your sides and slip under the wire and over the stones.

Behind us the wood settles again. The squirrel is down, scampering out from the bottom of the tree. The magpie disports himself across the floor and the rabbit slowly ventures out of his burrow. He pops up on to the bank, jumps down again, bumps a yard or two towards the ferns and comes back. It is a sort of stock taking. He sniffs the air, listens and waits for a sight of his neighbour before going back to the drystone wall, across the damp ground where he will leave his tracks beside those of the blackbird. The pigeon hen returns to her chick, that half-haired, half-feathered, blue-skinned, cold-looking creature that crouches on the platform of sticks, keeping company with the addled egg. Somehow the mother bird alights and covers her shivering offspring.

Down in the heart of the little planting the pheasant materialises. There is no other word for his reappearance. One minute the brown slope running to the blackberry is bare and the next the pheasant is there, softly, gently, the slightest movement of a stalk of grass. He walks a stately pace or two, his tail sweeping the ground, halts, listens. The

bright eye moves, the blood-red comb and head feathers rise and the tail lifts as he goes on, pecking at some tiny insect as he goes. What shades of blue, and chestnut brown, and that neck ring, like the brand on the wood pigeon, the mark on the grass snake. The sounds of the wood are sounds he knows, the stone rocking as a rabbit bobs over into the moss, the scolding of the squirrels, the sharp scorn of the jay.

The wood comes to life, but the grass snake calls it a day. Perhaps she has enjoyed her last bit of summer warmth, for a lethargy is infecting her. The first little whisper of a cooler breeze, the hand of winter, so hard to detect, is putting just a degree of coldness in the earth. The sun's heat has gone a fraction earlier than it did yesterday and the leaf has changed a shade from dark green to lighter green, a thing so slight that it seems that the leaf is not dying but that the light on its surface is getting brighter, here in the depths.

The love-talk of the pigeons is in vain. There will be no new brood in the fir top, for in the evening, when the little wind rustles the ears of corn, there is a mist in the lower branches. Tonight, with less warmth and no insect life in the air, the bat does not fly. He hangs in his roost, feeling that same sadness that infects the snake, and he squeaks mournfully to his companions. The roosting birds come in, the animal life goes out. Soon, at dusk, the hillside will be alive with the rabbit population. The stoats will scurry along the dikeside, hunting the mouse or the young rabbit, and from the deep shadows of the gorse the hedgehog will come on her search for grubs and insects. It is almost dark and the owls glide down through the fields, the barn owl carrying her prey about, to and fro, to and fro in the gloom, seeming to wait for it to die in the powerful clasp of her claws. The vagrant, poaching collie dog hunts his way over the hill. A hundred blurred outlines make for the wood, bounding across the ditch and through the thorn hedge. The owl cries and its mate answers.

This is the little planting as it was, cliff-ended, sombre at nightfall, mysterious at daybreak. Here I had more adventures than anywhere. Here I went to hunt for rabbits, pigeons, or game for the harvesters' dinners, and here I skulked when the family toiled with hayrakes before a gathering storm. Along the woodside I snared and netted, stalked a stoat and robbed him of his prey. Always when I had to go back to school in England I made a last visit to this place and stood awhile, getting its topography fixed in my mind so that next time I came I knew that here a tree was missing and the gale had pushed over another shallow-rooted fir.

Less than three hundred yards separate the little planting from the 'high wood', although standing in one it is impossible to see the other, for the brow of the hill blocks the way. The connecting link between the two is the dike, coming up from the back of the hill and the high wood and then down the steep slope to a gateway, on into the hollow, along the ditch, among the ferns and bracken shoots to the march wall and the little planting's edge. On one side of the dike the bracken is never allowed to rise, but is scythed down before it manages to get to full height, a practice that produces a stunted bracken, no higher than a rabbit on its back legs. The other dike runs from the back of the little planting, up the edge of the moss, shouldering the tall gorse, away round the back of the hill, connecting with the wood by means of a bank and a hedge. Undulating and uneven, this dike, a march wall, all the way, for march walls are always higher, more strongly constructed to keep out a neighbour's sheep and cattle.

On warm summer days I often saw the squirrel on the dike. There was no doubt about the animal being a squirrel, I saw him too often and at too close a range to be mistaken, although I admit there were both stoats and weasels living at stations in the dike. A stoat is as fond of a home among the stones as a snake, but to see a squirrel there was always exciting. He was on a journey. When pursued he abandoned the top of the wall, got down and went bounding along on the blind side – the squirrel is a master in the use of cover and dead ground. He was invariably on his way to the low planting, or back from it to the high wood. What made him set out on that long treeless journey? For while the woods are not so far apart the journey along the stones is three or four times as long as that across the field as the pigeon goes. What told him that the other wood was there behind the hill? What made him set out – a shortage of food, a desire for some new aspect? Surely one pine top looks like another? Surely it was less tiring to stay at home? Perhaps some venturesome ancestor found his way along the stones, across that open country to the high wood, and left the knowledge to his family. I often wondered whether the voyager might not have been some unmated male or female, some less pugnacious one, driven out by the rest. Year after year I saw one or two along the stones. Their agility probably saved them from being preyed upon. In the open they could scurry and scuttle about with that springy, tender-footedness, but, like the stoat and weasel, the squirrels have no speed and are really slow movers. If I managed to cut one off, he at once disappeared, seeming not to hesitate to take advantage of the holes, dodging me somehow and then reappearing fifty yards away. As far as I could tell, the voyagers went unmolested by the stoat and the weasel, skipping round the odd thorn tree growing in the dikeside, winning their way to the new wood, adventurers oblivious to the view down there, across the country, the farms, whitewashed and sprawling, home paddocks and grazing, turnip fields, potato fields, fields of corn stretching back beyond the river, away

to the haze in the distance where the hills reared up and showed a rocky face or two. Out there, more than once, I had seen the eagle soaring in long slow circles, so high that they were dots in the summer sky, so unbelievable that I always passed my hand across my eyes in case they were not birds in the distance but midges close at hand.

When I was small, I scaled every climbable tree in the little planting. I climbed in early spring to examine the rookery, to inspect the nest of the carrion crow or the magpie, and in the summer to put my hand into a squirrel drey. The squirrel likes a fork in a tree. His home is an ill-designed affair, looking like a bundle of dead twigs and beech leaves, a sort of accident, a thing you could mistake for sticks falling and gathering in the crotch of a tree. The first time I found one I felt sure it was a bundle of twigs blown into the fork or fallen there from a higher tree, and yet, no other tree was close at hand. I was only too willing to climb up to investigate, but the thing that excited me was the fact that I was sure that there was movement in the sticks. Up I went, slithering, slipping, clambering and making the tree shake, but keeping my eyes always on the twigs. As I climbed the last yard I decided that I had been mistaken. I thrust my hand into the sticks. It was a sort of nest. It had a roof, a slightly hollowed cavity with another exit. As my hand went in, the structure shook and three squirrels came out in a hurry. A fourth, hustled and balked in his escape by the others perhaps, nipped my finger. I almost fell out of the tree. All four went bark-clawing up the branch less than a foot from my face, and one after another launched themselves across a gap of several feet to the next tree. By the time I was back on the ground they were out of sight. No doubt they were aloft there somewhere, watching me, gripping the trunk with their powerful claws, motionless, head down or head up, peering round branches or straight into the abyss at the bottom of which I stood with head and face upturned.

I remember being told not to thrust my hand into holes in the ground or holes in drystone walls, or, for that matter, into the nests of birds. This was after I had related my experience with the squirrels, but such advice was little heeded. Within yards of the little planting's edge there were always four or five rabbit 'nests'. By carefully uncovering these I was able to study the development of the young rabbit. The wild rabbit doe leaves the warren to have her young, afraid, it is said, of the cannibal tendencies of her mate. In the field she digs a burrow about a yard long and close to the surface, lines it with grass and fur plucked from her flanks, and has her young. They are born blind, hairless and blue in colour, fumbling, groping, helpless little creatures. The mother protects them by scraping the earth over the mouth of the burrow, making such a thorough job that it is hard to detect the entrance. She continues to close the hole after suckling the young until they are furred and almost ready to leave. Going to one of these burrows less blocked than usual, my brother thrust his arm in, only to withdraw it again hurriedly, for a stoat had fixed itself to his hand. The savage little beast had entered the burrow, filled himself with the blood of the helpless young and was sleeping off the effects of his orgy when disturbed. Off he went across the turf, vanishing in the heap of stones at the planting's end. My brother, a little daunted and dismayed, sucked his hand where the stoat's sharp teeth had pierced his flesh. A little while later, at the back end of the year, I shot a stoat at this place and pondered the brutal ways of nature, for he was in his winter coat, white and conspicuous, visible a quarter of a mile away. There was no snow on the ground, for the coat of the stoat, brother to the ermine, changes with the season and not with the weather. He will be brown on a March snow, white on the green and brown of a field in November. When the coat changes to white he seems a much more lithe, alert little beast than when in his brown and fawn. He stops to look at man, goes out of sight, comes back, the epitome of

curiosity, takes a second look, pauses with one foot raised, rears up, then skips to cover again. The sight of him always makes me shiver. The keepers never call a truce in their war against him, but round the farm, so long as there are rats, he is always spared. Yet, I do not fancy him as a great killer of rats. He is game enough when after the little mouse, when his musky odour is paralysing the rabbit into crouching and waiting for its end. I fancy that a rat dies too hard for the stoat. I have seen rats fastened to the neck and lips of a dog, fighting as the dog killed them one by one. The stoat, like his smaller relative, the weasel, is a sly hunter, a master of viciousness among the pheasant chicks and the blind rabbits, but too cunning and crafty to fight for his meal. Watch him hunting, up above ground from one burrow to the next, a sniff at the air, a look round and down he goes. He spends an age below. What terror he spreads only he knows, but often a rabbit will bolt or quietly pop out and sit on the bank, already feeling that strange rigour in his limbs. No blind end remains unexplored, for he is as thorough in his search as the ferret. Waiting for him to reappear one can imagine the rabbit colony hastening on through the network, each one terrified of turning into a cul-de-sac.

Out he comes, gliding up the bank, through the grass like a tiger, and yet so silent that he is no more than a shadow. His keen eyes and nose miss nothing. The rabbit that sat above the burrow has moved on. Now it is in a smaller warren in the next bank. This is the one he will eventually hound out into the open. This poor creature knows its end already. The stoat seems to know it too. In half an hour, maybe sooner, maybe longer, it will all end out there, just across the ditch in the lush grass. The stoat takes his time, works his way on through the galleries, through the roots, past the buried and protruding stones. The doomed quarry comes out. It is hunched, different from any of its fellows. It does not run. All it needs is that wonderful spurt it had when it darted into the wood last night, but a change has taken place. Some gland has operated perhaps. The power to run has gone. When it moves only a little faster, the stoat is scuttling after it. They reach the grass. The pitiful squealing begins, frightening every small creature in the wood. The stoat is clinging there at the back of the rabbit's neck, taking its life in greedy gulps that stain his mouth crimson. The rabbit lives a little while, the stoat lies by its side, doing its awful work. A sort of sleepiness comes over the prey. If you rushed to save it now the stoat would run a yard or two and then watch you, but the rabbit would die. It began to die back there in the burrow when that strange thing happened to its muscles and its will to escape.

It has always been a source of wonder to me that the population of the wood can live together, the greedy magpie, the jay, the carrion crow, the kestrel or the hawk, the stoat and the weasel with all the non-preying, harmless animals and birds. In the little planting's length it provides homes and nesting places for most of these. Only the fox and the badger are missing. Weasels abound along the dikeside. Once I stood still while at least eight chased each other in line, crossing my feet twice, and running round me more than once, making me think of those old stories of the countryside about man being attacked by hordes of hunting weasels. This family was at play, I feel sure, unless the leader had some titbit in his mouth. When my fear left me, I seized a stone from the dike and hurled it into the little gorse bush into which they had just disappeared. One darted out, another scuttled up the bank and went through a small hole in the dike and I was alone, breathing more freely, aware of the blood in my ears, and having that reaction that made me wish I had a gun in my hands. When a similar thing happened many years later – this time three stoats raced round me – I shot them, killing two with one shot and the third with the second barrel. Like other stoats I have shot, they gave off a nauseous odour as they died. The keeper would have awarded me a medal that day, and probably have taken it back before night, for what is a man to do when a cock grouse and three hens sail in over the wall only thirty yards ahead?

Jeck came to work for the family before I was born. We had a good few poachers among our ploughmen and stablemen. Jeck was one of the most active poachers, the least active ploughmen. He looked round with a knowing eye. He missed nothing, the pheasant in the turnips, the hare on the hill. On his first day he heard the black cock cackling on the moss. He could not believe his eyes when he saw the rabbit tribe feeding out from the side of the little planting. He told me afterwards that the little planting could not have been put there to cover pheasants at all, but as the answer to a longnet-man's dream. It had everything the net man prayed for, a smooth hillside, good feeding. There was nearly always a little wind along the hollow. Jeck brought his net and reduced the tribe. The first night he went, the catch was so great that when he came to lift his coupled pairs he knew he could never carry them home. Taking a few, he strode across the fields to the farm, cleaned the midden barrow at the pump, and wheeled it back for his catch. I do not know how much the dealer paid him, certainly not the seven and sixpence I see they are asking today, but Jeck probably finished up so drunk that he was useless for days. The rabbits of the little planting were prolific, however, and if Jeck did not take them all it was because he had the human weakness for wanting the forbidden. He always wanted to go where he was not permitted to go. He was a poacher because, as he said, his mother had slept with a poacher. Others, however, came to the little planting. Everyone at home knew they were there.

'Poachers on the hill tonight,' someone would observe after going out to inspect the sky and the moon ploughing the clouds. 'Lamps going to and fro' yonder. The keeper in his bed. He knows when to show face and when not to.' Sometimes a dog yelped up the dusky hollow, or on a quiet night we would hear the sound of a stick snapping and the sound echoed in the wood was carried to us by some freakishness of the atmosphere.

I have confessed, elsewhere, to having taken to poaching when I was small. I took to an ancient double-barrelled shotgun when I was twelve, and have it yet, a shaky heirloom from the side of the grandfather clock in the farm kitchen. When I had it repaired by a fashionable gunsmith some years ago, he did the job and referred in his bill to 'this ancient weapon'. This gun took me into the little planting. It is true I had snared the runs and entrances and had gone in hoping to knock down a pheasant with a stick, but armed with the gun I began to poach in earnest. A famous Glasgow firm made my gun. It has what are known as Damascus barrels of soft steel that dents easily. Once it had two artistically shaped hammers, but one got lost. What old farm gun ever has a pair of matched dogs? Its locks are scrolled, its barrels figured, its fore-end is a piece of sweet-smelling wood, cedar, I think. Alas, its stock is not the stock I once cradled to my cheek. The stock got snapped when Bill or Harry showed us how he drilled in the army, and has been replaced with a new stock of lighter wood. I have not used it since, for my inclination to stand and stare has almost completely overcome my desire to shoot. When I first had this wonderful gun I went to the little planting. I knew the hazards. A man shoots one day and when he comes out the next, someone is hiding up for him. I began to rise at daybreak, before daybreak, so that by the time I reached the little wood day was only half arrived. Now that I recall those expeditions I know that half the zest was in the morning air; that freshness, that peewit call, that ghostly flight of gulls in the grey sky that made me wonder if they had spent the night up there; that faraway call of the curlew, a sound that has made me stand still in the heart of London, transported in time and place.

It is never easy to identify the stuff of one's enjoyment, the exact combination of light and shade, texture, emotion, circumstance, that lifts the heart and makes things fixed in time. To tell you what a hundred expeditions to the little planting at daybreak held for me would need all the years they have encompassed. The dew on my boots, the wind of the morning in my face and the old gun in my hands, stumbling over the uneven field, passing through a cobwebbed gap, hearing sounds made a score of miles away, a milk train in a cutting, someone clattering churns, wheels on a hard road, the faint piping of the creamery whistle. The family, early risers though they were, did not always know I was out. I opened the door cautiously, trod softly on the gravel and stole away to the wicket gate. The shadows swallowed me as I headed for the thorn hedge, the gap in the gorse, the spars of the gate. It might be so cold that I caught my breath. The frost might scatter before my boots as I disturbed the grass, but every step filled me with greater happiness. The snipe rose in the hollow, made their stone-scraping noise and vanished, a waterhen hurried back for the shelter of the ditch. It mattered very little that I had two cartridges and no more. The morning might be too wonderful to be disturbed. Sometimes I came back, drunk with all I had seen, empty-handed and ravenous for my breakfast, with little bits of the wood fast to my clothes, a strand of that weed we called sticky willie, the burrs of the burdock, a fragment of bracken that had worked its way down between my sock and my boot.

'I saw the horned owl this morning,' I would announce.

We had a horned owl, a stuffed one, on the parlour mantelpiece. He was too beady-eyed to be real. Too moth-eaten as well, I fear. Once, thinking it was my duty to replace him, I lifted my gun to an owl in the wood and brought him back in triumph. He would soon be on the mantelpiece when the taxidermist had finished with him. My aunts were horrified. This was a crime worse than poaching. It was worse than a crime, it was bad luck. Grandfather was due in for his breakfast. At that moment he was crossing the court. In no time at all he would be in the kitchen, standing there without saying a word, but preparing a reprimand that would show he was shocked, his feelings hurt, my rating falling fast and bringing his grey hairs in sorrow. My aunts looked about. They hated scenes and sermons. They glanced at the ceiling, in the way of praying, I suppose, and saw the pan basket hanging there on its hook. With the scraping of a chair, a flurried confusion in which a lecture was delivered, they put the owl in the basket, whisked my breakfast out of the oven and had me at my usual place at the table. The thing was forgotten. It was a brilliant morning, with the sun coming up across there beyond the old stackyard, the leaves of the two elm trees fluttering in the breeze. It was easy for everyone to forget. The thing was completely forgotten. One day it became apparent that all was not well in the kitchen. One of my aunts was not blessed with a keen sense of smell. To her fell the task of preparing a hare for the pot or doing any of those less pleasant tasks in the kitchen. She had, nevertheless, a horror of the smell she was incapable of detecting. Let anyone else say that something was off and she left no dish uninspected, no tureen lid unlifted, no corner undisinfected. The search for the cause of the odour went on. It was not successful.

'Dear me, in my kitchen!' they remarked to those who could stay long enough to comment.

The awful breeze greeted everyone at the door. Even the dog deserted his place beneath the table, and, poor dog, he had been treated to a bath. I am sure my aunts aged a little from that day. Unfortunately, I was away. Nearly a week passed before the decomposing bird was discovered. What relief. What awful, unvoiced accusations had been on the point of being uttered. What disinfecting and thanksgiving followed!

Looking out of the window, across the sows' field, you can see the dock bending in the wind, the thistle pointing after the flowing clouds, the leaves going one after the other from the branches of the ash tree. The afternoon is young, but it is one of those days that are full of winter and the sad signs of decay complete. The wind is the thing. Stand at the door and hear what it does to the giant elm over there, hear the waves on the invisible shore, or go with wind-plucked clothes to the garden just to listen to that sound in the pine trees, the hushing and shrieking through the hedge. Do these things and think of the wood pigeon and the little planting. The sound up there is a thousand times the thrashing and swaying of the elm top; a million flecks of leaves and husk are showering out of the wood, and in all this crescendo the pigeon is deafened, made less aware of his danger, although his alertness never leaves him for so much as the blinking of his watchful eye. You can go now to the little planting and wait for him. When you go, you cross the black potato field, the rushy hollow, and jump the flooded burn. Say nothing, for the wind will have the words from your lips before your companion can hear them. In the side of the trees there is shelter, a haven where the wintering beast stands in the remnants of straw and turnip feed scattered there yesterday. The trees nod, the thorn hedge shivers. The wood welcomes as it welcomed the first hunter ever to go among the trees.

There should be a word for the flight of pigeons, more than a word, a phrase for all the beauty of movement that is theirs. Perhaps there is, but to me the birds coming in to settle are a wheeling of pigeons, a glide, a sailing. A glide of pigeons, yes, for at that very moment when they

are about to settle, with only a yard or two to go, they are a glide, and then a fluttering of pigeons. Perhaps in the tree tops they are an alert of pigeons, certainly, when they go they are an alarm or a clattering.

In the shelter of the little planting it is not so cold. With this high wind, anyone could be stealing up on us, half a dozen others keeping us company undetected. The wind covers it all, roaring, sighing, blustering, shaking drops of rain out of the needles of the pine, thrusting its fingers through the holes among the stones of the dike. The rabbit stays below, snug in the warren, dozing the wild day through. Perhaps he will show up about dark, nipping out across the ditch to nibble a blade of grass within the wood's shadow. The hare is away in his form in the lee side of a dike, or in some shallow, undraughty hollow over which the wind streams, carrying stalks and fragments of stubble, shrivelled hay, the seeds of a hundred grasses and weeds. In the moss the grouse are huddled in the peat bank, close to the humps of gorse, the heather combed out above them, a brood of moor chickens. Somewhere in the little planting the pheasant, too, is sitting, ready to run through the undergrowth or steal quietly away. If driven into the open, he will rocket up and roll across the tops of the trees.

We have come to do that thing this day is made for, to wait for pigeons, and hope that they will fly before the day dies and the wood is left to the misery of the storm and the disconsolate owl. Wrap your old coat about you, all manner of things are to be seen when the wood is rocked by the wind and you stand motionless. The stoat's hunt is longer. His quarry escapes him because the scent is snatched from before his nose. The crow sits in contemplation, the rooks crowd in the thick trees and a whirring, anxious flock of starlings takes refuge almost above us. Have patience. It takes circumstances of one sort and another to make the pigeons fly in this wind. In the faraway wood behind the cottage an old man goes fumbling for kindling and breaks a stick. The sound is sharp and clear in a lull in the wind and a pigeon rises to lead the flock away, or, in another wood, a ploughboy takes a wild shot at a bird or a rabbit and puts all the pigeons into the wind. Somewhere in a little wood on the top of a hill, an open place where two or three horses stand with their sterns to the gale, the wind becomes so fierce that the small birds leave, like a shower of dead leaves themselves, and then the pigeons depart too, turning a wing to the current, slicing down to shelter and then beating over the countryside towards us. They come now, like fish in a great deep, clear lake, rising in flight, sinking, floundering a little, struggling heavily up the hill, battling their way through the hollow, always into the mouth of the wind and never with it, unless in fear. In fright, chased by the peregrine, who can outfly them easily, or speeding before a hail of shot, they will go with the wind so fast into the distance that their size will shrink like a bee flying into a summer sky. Now, on the brow of the hill, they rise, an invasion flight, black dots on the skyline, driven up as they meet a new blast of air, but beginning to struggle down to the cover and shelter of the little planting.

Stand still. Let the branches screen your face. Make no movement, even if one seems in range. Let nothing hasty betray us, for there are two shots here, coming and turning away. They are wheeling in through the clearing, turning, a brief sailing. Now put up the old gun. The gunshot was oddly muffled. See what happens there: the flight parts, one bird hesitates, wings outstretched, and then, the control of wings gone, begins to tumble out of the air. Let it lie in the dead bracken. The sound has gone on the wind, a quarter of a mile away and lost. Two birds have turned out to go with it, for they felt the shot cross their path, but the rest are oddly unwary or reluctant to fly on. They are swinging round, a bit ragged, a straggler or two, but they are beating along the wood and coming back over our heads. They are a little high. One flaps out of the formation and alights, a tired bird. The rest go round and plane in once more, back to the same group of trees. Here they are. Pigeon pie tomorrow. This time the wind falls just as the gun fires. For an awful moment the wood's heart misses a beat, and then pigeons we had not suspected were there take flight and go out over the hill. The starling flock rises, the crows flap out and use their wings to glide off. The rooks rise like gnats. A kind of telegraph takes this warning across the countryside. Now a bird that was coming in on a long straight flight changes direction a degree or two and passes three hundred yards to our left. Scanning the sky we can see this bird making a long turn. He is off to the farthest hills, to some place where he will roost tonight. In a new perching place, for they have not yet settled for the day, the flight we shot into flutters to the treetops, sitting along the branches in ones and twos, like smoky blue ornaments, silhouetted against the sky.

The wind is hardly more than a whisper now, but the wren does not sing. No bird sings. No sound is in the little planting save the rubbing of crossed branches, and a whispering in the bracken the wind has so lately been lashing. Put your back against the tall pine and examine your birds. Did you ever see such fine condition? The sheen on the feathers tells you that these are healthy birds, strong and active. Their crops are lumpy with acorns picked today. A week or two ago they were in one of the fine woods of the continent. Now, recovered from their migration, they are fat and round. What a shot they are. Some men will pretend they often put two down when they lift their gun, but, coming and going, they are not an easy shot, unless the shooter skulks in the trees and picks them off from their roost. A man who gets half he aims at does well enough.

We have shot our pigeons for a pie, so we will not go offering them to the dealer. Sixpence for a pigeon? Remember, we are in the little wood, twenty years ago. Sixpence a pair maybe, for, plump though they are, their flesh is dark and not always tender. They need boiling before they are roasted. They need stewing before they go into our pie. If the wind would only drop for the day and a little watery sun come out, we might take them to the place where the old cornstack once stood, propping their heads with a forked stick, making them lifelike with a few supporting twigs. In a little while they would be joined by one or two greedy relatives.

Once I made myself a pigeon with the grey lining of an old jacket, some wire and rag and a few daubs of paint. The garden might be in need of weeding, my path in full dandelion bloom and lawn six inches high, but such a thing has always absorbed my attention. When I was small I could trim a snare peg and forget my dinner, dabble my arms in a stream and forget my supper. This pigeon had the right sheen, the white ring on his neck, the little crust of white on his beak, the right shaped tail. He was a work of art. I wish I knew how to tie a fly as well. I popped him in my bag and set off for the fields. It was wonderful to see how this ragbag bird lured others from their line of flight. His pitch was in a harvest field. I was thrilled to see it happen. They came round and settled, but somehow, I could not shoot them. I began to study the art of the decoy. Sit the bird with head down wind and I was making a mistake, for no pigeon feeds with its tail and feathers ruffled, but sit him on a stook, head up or head down, and in a few minutes I would

see birds a long way off changing direction to fly over the feeding decoy, take a soaring turn and come in to join him. It did not seem to matter that he was made of cloth and wire and rags. Once the live bird settled he sought greedily for food. Two birds brought a third, then a fourth.

I must admit that I once did cock my gun. It had been very warm and I sat among the corn and fell asleep. When I awoke I was startled to see a pigeon within a few yards, my decoy, which had fallen from the stook!

I came very near to destroying him with a blast of five shot. He was so lifelike. It was possible to bend the body into the most natural postures. The trouble with the scheme was that when I went out with my decoy I came home without pigeons. One day my spaniel pup took a delight in shaking the stuffing out of him. In a little while he was no more. It was saddening to see my cunning strewing the path. I began to shoot pigeons once more with the approval of the farmer, who had been keeping an eye on my behaviour among his stooks of wheat.

He accosted me as I was going up to the field one sunny evening. 'I'm glad to see you have given up bringing the birds to my field,' he informed me. 'A bushel of wheat I must have lost there! Permission to shoot it was you asked for. On Saturday last you had them all round you and never fired a shot!'

It was so true I was ashamed. That evening I shot more than usual to salve my conscience.

But we were there in the little planting with the cones falling from the trees. Dusk is coming. There seems to be half an hour or so when birds come into their roosting places. There is light on the top of the wood, but gloom below. A settling bird peers down, short-sightedly, nervously. It moves to another branch and sits with neck stretched. You may shoot a crow or a mistle thrush now, unless you know your birds, for the gloom and the black screen of twigs is deceiving. The pigeon listens and watches without relaxing until the gloom is so thick about it that you could not distinguish its outline well enough to take aim. A man who knows birds can tell them at roost or in flight two or three miles away. He can tell pigeons, rooks, peewits, curlews and starlings at the extremity of his vision. They are all distinctive in the manner of their flight. The roving formation is a gathering of rooks, the undulating, air-manoeuvring birds are peewits, the bustling cloud is a flock of starlings. No one ever has an excuse for shooting a homing pigeon by mistake, for they have a lightness, a speed, an economy of flight that marks them apart from all others of the family. They fly with purpose, less light-heartedly than the flights of stock doves that sweep down on to the stubble, in over the elms to take a brief rest in the firs. Stock doves are less wary in the trees than the wood pigeon, quicker to fall to a shot, for they are smaller birds. You can tell them at once by the green sheen. They have no white ring. They are neat little birds, not unlike those in the dovecote. When shot they tumble easily and hardly ever make a recovery in the air as the wood pigeon sometimes does, for their quills are not as strong and perhaps their breast feathers are not so thick to turn the pellets of lead.

The shadows are growing in the little planting. We have to crawl out, risking a wetting in the half-choked ditch. As we go squelching along the hollow a bird calls in the darkness. The owl has it to himself tonight. A little squall of rain is gusting out of the south-west. The light of the oil lamp shows in the farmhouse window. Supper will be on the hob. It will be warm beside the peat fire and you can be sure we shall be dozing before the evening is half through.

You have been to the little planting in the dusk and know it in the early day. In winter it stands shouldering the gale across the moss. Once the moss itself was a wood. The years will make a peaty strip of the little planting itself. Every winter another tree falls to the gale. One lists, another goes crashing down, raising a great network of roots and a wall of black soil. In the drier months the soil hardens and a rabbit makes its bed in its shelter, a neat little form that you might stare at for a minute or two without seeing him. A weed begins to grow where the tree stood. A clump of foxgloves may appear, or a wood anemone shows its pale face on the exposed earth. Among the fibrous roots a thrush or a blackbird begins to build. Some of the shallow roots are only folded. The tree grows on. It cannot grow horizontally, but its branches that are vertical revive and grow like small trees. The spruce has not this tenacity. Usually when it falls it dies. The light twigs moulder, the stronger ones snap, the surface of the wood gradually makes a grave for the spruce. Others, more hardy, grow on, blossom and seed, and make a barrier through which the woodbine or the briar may grow. Moss coats the trunk of the fallen tree, and in the nest at its base the bird lays her eggs and raises her brood. Often I have seen more than one nest there. The little nest of the tit or wren, the great grass-lined basin of the blackbird. These things you have yet to see in the little planting in the spring, for a score of families are raised here in that bright, happy light of the young year, when the lambs are bleating and growth is beginning everywhere. No birds are earlier in the little planting than the rooks and the carrion crows. The first mellow light has the carrion crow building, bringing in his materials, the living twigs, the wisps of sheep's wool, the strand of binder twine, the fragment of newspaper. In this countryside, where a shot through the nest often ends it all, the crows always seem to be making nests in new sites, abandoning the old ones.

Watch the carrion crow. We have all the days of the spring to watch him, from the day he sails in with his mate until the day he and his family go off to scavenge together.

There is probably no more intelligent member of the family of crows than the carrion crow. The rook is bright-eyed and perky, the jackdaw has a jauntiness, the magpie his impudence and the raven his legal air, but the carrion crow has cunning beyond them all. He is not afraid of man. He swerves to avoid him when he has a gun, flies over him when he has none. The carrion crow comes to the little planting late in the

day. He and his mate are sailing in to settle on the very tip of the tree. Like small editions of the smith's raven, these two, and they have a fine sheen to their feathers. The air is cold. A frost is in the wood making the mud of the ditch congeal. The crow calls three times and then he is silent. Up in the wood the hoarse call sounds, marking the waning of the afternoon. Early today this pair shared a mouse, then went off to the pullet run, perching to look round, flying down to steal. What a pair of thieves they are, side-hopping to the trough, snatching a morsel, going back to the post. They have a knowing way with them. This game is in their blood. They were doing it a thousand years ago. Someone comes and they are off, but in no undignified haste. A few heavy wingbeats, low across the grass and up, up, cawing, agreeing to come to the little planting, and here they are.

In the morning, a warm sun having risen, driving the frost back through the wood, they decide to stay. It is time to be about the business of setting up house in the slender fork. The building begins and continues day by day. Out they go to feed, to gather materials. Back they come, up out of the hollow, across the wood to the nesting site, their shadows skimming the ground as they fly in sunlight. At the end of the day the male bird gives those three or four throaty caws. Beneath them in the wood the blackbirds fight for territory. The eggs are laid when the oats are being sown, about the time when the peewit is nesting. Four or five more crows arrive in the world. Five more crows to forage the countryside, to pick the eyes of the sickly lamb, the snared rabbit, to steal the eggs from the outlying hen house or hang about the potato field pecking the potatoes that protrude, green-sided, from the set-up rows. Seven birds in the early summer and then, before autumn, one is fluttering on a pole in the field, a stinking corpse, and another is shot at the hen run where he has been to help himself to the young chicks. In the little planting the nest weathers and in the following season the horned owl, the long-eared owl of the firwood, will consider its amenities.

When the crow is nesting, the rook, too, is in the low planting's rookery. You could almost step from one tree top to the other and every top has its nest, although all are not breeding nests. There they are, the eggs of a brood that will strip half the turnip hill in their search for the wireworm or the pout grub, toddling unsteadily along the furrows and doing their work of drawing the plants as thoroughly as some of the schoolboys hired to do thinning. Most of the fields have a scarecrow, but these are rooks. You can tell them by their bald fronts, that bare patch at the base of their beaks. You can tell them in flight because they are garrulous, a joyful congregation, flying light-heartedly across the countryside, making a sound that is part of early summer itself. Have you ever eaten rook pie? The flesh is as white as that of any chicken. The farmer sometimes has rook pie. When he shoots he puts the whole tribe into the air with such a chorus of cawing that a labourer two miles away turns his head to stare.

I remember climbing to the little planting's rookery when I was no more than six or seven years old. I remember, too, my brother climbing a very tall tree in the rookery and falling out of it. As he fell, branch after branch crashed down with him. The sound of his falling was like a rushing train. He crashed at my feet on the breadth of his back, his breath gone, his life gone, I thought for a moment. The surface of the little planting was soft, however. He rose a minute later, a little shaky and white-faced, and spat something out of his mouth.

'I'll never go up there again,' he vowed, and it was an easy vow, for he had stripped the old tree of almost every foothold. All he suffered, apart from shock, were a few scratches and a broken, half-addled egg in his mouth.

If we leave the little planting now, it will only be to go to another wood, and there are woods all round us in this rolling country, woods that have names, woods that thrust their pine spears into the sky and stand in solid ranks, woods that crowd the grey roads, woods that are silent and brooding, and others that are alive with the sounds of streams that pass through them. We are going to them all, for I want to take you stalking a hare in a wood, to glimpse the deer in the forest moor, the badger in the Welsh wood just a mile away, and the fox too. If you know

how to make crab apple jelly, or wine from the fruit of the bullace tree, come with me. Come with me to see the woodcock, the treecreeper, and nuthatch. If you are not afraid of a dish of mushrooms that were picked in a wood, or if you are in need of a faggot of kindling, we shall be in such a spot tomorrow, gathering a bag of hazelnuts or a basket of giant blackberries.

Come to the high wood, uphill out of the hollow where the hawthorns stand by the ditch, uphill out of the evening mist and the shadows. All at once, for a little while, the sun makes our faces golden and we stop to hear the nightjar calling, for in the shoulder of the hill, in the long shadows, it is already night. We stand only a minute or two and day fades on our faces, flowing away into the west, dissolving before our eyes like snow in the stream. The world is left to that strange half-light that is summer night in the north. What a time of mystery and magic this is. We see the folds of the hills black, the ridge where the trees mark the sky and a light twinkling away in the distance, the yellow glow of a cycle lamp wobbling and twisting, vanishing and reappearing along a road that is only marked by this journeying countryman, pedalling his way home to a cottage or to some assignment at a finger-posted crossing. What shadows obscure the faces and forms of the children that greet him in the gloom of his garden and yet he knows them, or, if he is young and travelling to his sweetheart, he has only to stop in this drowsy silence to hear her sigh in the leaves of the ash tree. How kind is the gloaming, for it softens and makes beautiful the whole universe and the girl is a goddess in its light.

Over the brow of the hill. Do you hear the bird singing in the high wood? Down below it is dark, night among the elderberry bushes and the blackthorns. Summer night in the high wood, warm and alive. In the little patch of sky the leaves of the beech look black and flutter gently. Out on the turnip field it is impossible to see the rabbit or the hare but the leaves rustle and tremble, the yellow weeds sway. The night is full of the little sounds that mark the season, the flying beetle's note as it goes off speeding through the gloom, the cry of lambs on the grass hills, a restless dog barking in the hollow drum of a barn or a cartshed, the faraway and yet weirdly near sound of two countrymen talking at a road end. The bird sings and some oddness in the air makes its heart happy. The last combing of day goes from the sky and the bird is silent. The owl calls. The wood sits brooding, sheltering its bird life, its millions of insects. The tawny owl flies, the wild cat hunts. Who has time in his life to discover how far the rabbit ranges at night, the territory covered by the hare? Who can tell what world the owl sees as he perches on the stump like a ghost, or why he does so when he is so lately out of roost, for night for him is day and day night? Does it become a brighter place of monochrome, like moonlight, and does he sit contemplating its beauty and peacefullness? One half of the world goes to sleep and the other half awakes. Here in the crumbling bank the wasp nest settles. It is not completely dormant. It is still alive, vibrating, humming gently. Part of the pattern of night and day, scavengers of sticky jampot shards and midden refuse, food for the badger, distraction for the honey bee, grubs for the hungry fish, a hot noon fury to warn the browsing beast away.

Out of the wood's edge comes the hedgehog, along the ditch a vole journeys and a rat from the stackyard goes on a voyage of discovery across the murky field. The weasel hunts the mouse and the mouse searches for the beetle. Another beetle buries the remains of the mouse by undermining the corpse, and the little owl lifts the mouse to find the beetle. What a pattern it all is. When the ground is frozen and the beetle is in its larval stage, the mouse sleeps. Perhaps the owl searches for the larva of the beetle instead of the carcass that would provide work for the unborn undertaker. Now, in summer, flies sleep under the leaves or roll in tireless little clouds beneath the branches, midges and gnats at exercise, horseflies and solitary wasps dozing until tomorrow's sun. A thousand thousand flies to feed the fat trout in the stream or make a breakfast for the swallow. Some will rise into the morning air and some sting the herd into high-tailed flight. The robin lives on a few of these countless insects, sharing them with the tits and the wrens, the hedge sparrows and a dozen others, all of them asleep in this vast world of twigs and stems and leaves through which the night air steals and a little breeze whispers. The chaffinch hen is incubating in the tip of the down-swept larch bough, the goldfinch out in the scrub where blackthorn, briar and bramble make a wall of defence. In this place, at harvest and after, you will hear the tinkling music of the goldfinch flock, see the painted marvel of blood-red head and butter-yellow wing marks. In the shadow that is the stone heap and briar and bramble patch, the hen pheasant broods, in the top of the holly the magpies are crowding their nest, small enough for one, hopeless for four. Tomorrow they will change their habits and roost at night in the thorn tree, leaving the soiled nest to moulder and be shaken to pieces in next winter's gales.

In the stones the adder moves, for there is warmth in the ground tonight. The adder, too, has been searching for his food among the helpless creatures that over-populate the bank of the cornfield. This is the dark-skinned short adder that killed the collie pup, biting him in the lip; the adder that fell from the hayfork on the other side of the stone wall before the field was clover. Out in the clover the rabbits jump and run. The purple blossoms bob, the leaves hiss. The world of the night belongs to these creatures, for the courting servant girl has gone home to bed, sighed her last romantic sigh and turned her flushed face into her pillow. In her kitchen the steels of the range are cooling fast and the clock's chimes mark the passing of the night more frequently than the barking dog, but muffled and gentle.

We should have gone to the high wood in daylight. You have not seen its tallest trees, the tops of its elms thrusting above the brow, its trees of ash and sycamore, beech, birch and oak, for the high wood is older and has only a few firs and pines. It is true that along the stream's edge the larch grows, its feathery branches screening the morning sky, its tough little leafy cones carpeting the ground. The long-coned spruce grows here too, but the deciduous trees outnumber the conifers ten to one. Here grow the elder, the blackthorn, the rowan and the hawthorn as well as the holly. The woodbine climbs the wall. The sloe bush needs only the stoniest corner, just a sour and damp bit of ground, like the elder. They make a barrier through which the largest animal hesitates to thrust itself. The roving ewe bounds into a clearing to escape a worrying dog and finds herself penned there, her wool combed by the thorns, her legs held fast by some tough and thick arm of a blackberry. She bleats once or twice. The flies gather on her eyes and nose. She ruminates while the sun climbs the sky and rolls down it again. Tomorrow or the day after, the shepherd will count and send his dog to make the foolish creature lunge and tear herself out of her prison.

The fruit of the high wood is the rowan, the sloe, the elderberry, the crab apple; jelly and wine, sharp and bitter, summer trapped in an old stone jar and let out after the passing of years; the popping of a cork, a heady fume from a cobwebbed bottle. Up here the squirrel has all the beech nuts he could wish for and at the end of the summer the acorns fall, the sycamore's winged seeds spin on to the stubble of the switchback hill, the ash keys rattle and rustle.

Look into the wood now, down through the trees. Right at the top there is a rabbit warren, a great community which you will never be able to count, for when a score are above ground four or five score are below. At daybreak a hundred run in the wood and on the field. The sun slips over the hills and shafts of light strike through the trees and you see rabbits everywhere, bounding into holes, bounding out, scuttling across mounds of red earth.

Slipping among the dikeside stones your foot breaks a sycamore limb and the breaking of the branch cracks in the wood to startle the magpies and make everything alert. The rabbits have gone and the morning sunlight splashes the ground. Did you hear the warning that every nervous buck gave to his neighbour? At the mouth of the burrow he bounced and beat the ground with his back legs so that the least wary of his relatives, coming through the short ferns or the nettles, had a second alarm. Away below, in the caverns of the warren, the whole tribe sits in tension. A rolling summer cloud races before the sun, its shadow darkening the corn hill and sweeping over the river like a ghost. There is a change in the wood, a breath of cool, almost chill air that makes the leaves shiver. The wren sings. Somehow the wren finds heart to sing at such times when the brightness of day is falling and the wood is a little sad.

We have not come to ferret the warren, for too many helpless youngsters live there and the grown rabbits do not bolt before the nip of the frost. We have come to look at the chaffinch, the master-builder in moss, hair and feather, the artist in shades of green and grey lichen from the stones. We have come quietly to this place where there is peace, undisturbed from morning to night, save when the stoat kills his prey, or the shrew warns the world of some frightened thing in the jungle of the long grass, where the blind worm is a monster slithering across the small stones. I can remember turning over a slab of rock – I was always doing such things to discover a toad or a nest of ants – and seeing the slow-worm for the first time. How he made me shiver: how snake-like he was. I had yet to learn that he was like the dragonfly, frightening to look at, shiver-provoking, but impotent. Perhaps the vibration of my coming made him prepare to slither away, or had he eyes in his skin? I did not fumble among the moss and stones to bring him back. Nature had made him snake-like for just that purpose.

We have come to look at the chaffinch, who has gathered beauty and put it all out at the end of a swaying limb, a tough limb of larch that has a few twigs into which the nest can be fixed. The hen is drab compared with her mate, but it is the hen who builds while the cock bird sings, and when all is said and done, it is beautiful: a painted bird singing, a nest so delicate, a piece of wool from a briar thorn, a feather from the hen run, the moss as green as it grows in spring, the grey lichen from those lichen-bearded stones on the hill all bound together with the cobwebs from the hayfield, and the branch gently rising and falling on the breeze through the wood. Four eggs, marled or stained a little as though they had been in a bilberry pie, and the hen bird sitting tight, crouching into her mossy nest, a sort of prayer that the brood will hatch, grow and fly without mishap, and then the larch tree can carry the woven moss and hair and wool until the twigs crumble into its bowl and the grey lichen darkens and dies. I never see the nest of the chaffinch without wondering at the little miracle of architecture it is.

Once I stood by a tree in which a chaffinch family were being raised. The nest was among small twigs on the side of the tree trunk. I was leaning against the tree watching a pigeon drinking at a pool when I became aware of the young birds. A strong wind was blowing and all four tried to crouch as far down in the nest as they could. Alas, there was only room for two. The wind blew first one out and then another. They tumbled at my feet. I stooped and picked them up. They were half-

fledged, clumsy, top-heavy little things, cold and uncomfortable. It took
me a few minutes to restore them to the nest. The four settled down for
a while, then began to twitter and quarrel and the same thing happened:
two birds fell to the grass. I looked carefully at them. As far as I could tell,
they were the same birds. The old law applying itself, but here, while the
wind lasted, I restored the balance. I gave the support of my hand to the
weak, back went the shivering pair. I watched from a knoll that enabled
me to overlook the nest. The wind blew, the four birds shuffled and
struggled. The two larger birds got down into the nest and the weaker
ones were forced on to their backs. The wind, and the discomfort they
caused their brothers, gradually brought them to that moment when
both toppled to the grass eight feet below. Again it happened, and again
I continued to put them back. The wind continued to blow. I could think
of nothing else to do, for once I had tried to save a wren chick by taking
it home and feeding it flies and tiny grubs, and had watched it die in a
very short time. This, it seemed, was a matter of waiting until the wind
abated, but the wind abated not, and at last I restored them to the nest
and hurried away. I could not wait to see the thing happen over again,
for I knew I would do no more than put them back. The following day
I passed by the tree. Two dead fledglings lay on the grass. Two live ones
sat snugly in the nest. The weak had gone to the wall; I sighed and went
away. Nature itself made and preserved the balance. That was why the
crow rifled the hen roost, why the sparrowhawk scouted the hedge in a
rapid twisting flight.

In the high wood in early summer, as in the low wood, or out in the
hayfield for that matter, there are countless hundreds of flies. Sit down
beneath a tree to rest and you will kill four or five at every slap of your
hand. Be so foolish as to draw from your pocket your snack of jam scone,
and you will kill ten times as many and a wasp or two for good measure.
I was in the high wood on a summer's morning to escape some tedious
chore, like going to the signpost to catch the grocer's van, or to the road-
end for the letters and the paper, when I discovered the bees. They were
domestic bees, not the brown wild bees, but ordinary bees from one

of our own colonies. They flew in a great exercising mass at the trunk of a tall tree. Cautiously I approached. They were 'our' bees, without doubt, for they were hostile. My grandfather had a way with bees, but he was the only member of the family who had, or even wished to have, such a gift. When he went to the hives he sometimes carried a smoker. Sometimes he remembered to put on his veil and keep it in place with his old 'hard' hat, but sometimes he could not be bothered to wait until such odds and ends were unearthed, particularly at the beginning of summer, when winter had rummaged them into the darkest corners of the farthest cupboards. I studied the bees from a fairly safe distance. One got in my hair and another made three or four mock attacks at my face. They were not a swarm on the move, but a colony in themselves. The tree had a small entry. Its inside was rotten or hollow. The bees were living in it like wild bees.

I carried the information home. My description of the bees was accurate. No one had any doubt that I had discovered a hive. Grandfather armed himself with all the tools and several others for good measure. Off we went to the high wood carrying a margarine box, a piece of rag, a smoker, a spray, a can, an axe and a dozen odds and ends twice the weight of a ferret and a set of nets. Grandfather set about the tree. I had hopes of a mouthful or two of fine clover honey, but the tree yielded no more than brood comb. It had not that blessing, a queen excluder, and as yet the hive had not started to set up anything like a winter store. We were after the queen, I discovered. Ten thousand swarmed about grandfather's head. He paused and picked them out from under his veil, combed one from his beard, gently lifted another from his eyebrow.

'This old veil has had the moths in it,' he said as he replaced his hat, but I was hardly listening. As the honey smell grew stronger the bees became more incensed. The sun came out. The heat became unbearable, the sound of buzzing more and more frightening. All at once, receiving two stings in rapid succession, and feeling at least half a dozen bees on various uncovered parts of my body, I turned and ran off down through the wood. The echoes boomed with grandfather's orders to

stand firm. At length I stood firm. I had had three or four more stings. I
went back towards the tree very cautiously. The air was thick with bees.
They made more noise than a reaping machine. They were prepared to
perish in defence of the queen and the brood. I bitterly regretted having
mentioned my discovery. I had one swollen eye and no morale at all
when grandfather came away. He sat down at a safe distance, where I
joined him.

'Now,' he said, 'if we're lucky they'll settle with the queen. If we're
unlucky they take off and we'll just have to take after them.'

We were unlucky. The queen came out from the inverted margarine

box, leaving the mass of brood comb. The colony joined her. Like a
cloud they went through the wood.

'Haste you with the water!' ordered grandfather.

The thing happened before I knew it. I fell and the water soaked into
the dry ground in a second or two. I got up and went sadly down to the
stream. I knew before I reached it that it was no more than the smallest
trickle, for the weather had been very dry.

'Water! Water!' grandfather shouted.

What was the use of hurry? I walked slowly back, past the tree in the
direction of the departing swarm.

'I've fallen with the can,' I shouted, 'and there's none in the burn.'

A sort of a contradiction, if you like, but I was hardly in a mood for choosing words. Just when the first tragic admonishing phrases came booming back at me, a bee that had been lurking somewhere for this particular moment flew up and stung me in the other eye. It would be as well, if you ever find bees in a wood, just to leave them there in peace.

Watch the hare in the middle morning when the sun is up and he begins to think of going to his form. We cannot tell how far he has gone by night, but now, when the sun is on the southern slope, oblique and yellow, touching the feathery grass, we can watch him coming back, for he is the hare from the high wood and he slips away in the bracken as silently as a partridge vanishing down a potato drill or a waterhen going into the rushes. We go with this hare to see him enter the wood, to see him settle and sleep. He belongs to the high wood, this tall, rusty-backed hare. He belongs as the kestrel belongs, making his home here for a season, escaping the snare, the yelping of dogs set after him on a Sunday afternoon, the poacher's gun. He is not young. Beneath his skin he carries a few pills of four or five shot. One of his soft brown ears is scarred with a shot wound. His family runs the hills and plains as far as the high bird's call sounds, and he knows every long furrow, every drain hollow, every dike hole and hedge gap, from here to the horizon. No stream roars in spate but he knows a place to cross; no ditch divides a moss but he can clear it at a bound as he races before the lurcher dog. All this is his country. He shares it with others, but it is his, fallow and arable, fir plantings and whin waste, mossy knowes and kingcup hollows. It is his, as it belongs to everyone who crosses it on a sunlit morning.

We went to catch this hare once with dog, net and gun. We waited for him in the shelter of the hedge and laid ambush at the gate, but now we want to see him come safely to the wood, for it is his shelter, as the cottage is the shelter of the ploughman. In March he will be gone, out over the hills, across the harrowed ploughing, mad, like all his kind, boxing on his hind legs, dancing that lunatic dance that is spring in the blood of a hare, or a bird or a man. He lives for March and March is in the shelter of the old bracken, the weak, overgrown grass, the faded dying garlic, the anemone leaves. March is in the wind that carries warning in sound and scent, in his living through the autumn and winter until the birds sing again.

He comes out through the spruce poles that bar the gateway, neatly, daintily, and he comes up in the sunlight from the place where the broken drain makes a bog in the turf, passing over the shoulder of the hill, skirting the docken patch. There is no hurry about his coming home. The sinews that can take him away with speed like the swallow's shadow are relaxed. He hops along on his strong back legs. His head is low, like a horse feeding in the pasture, and yet he is not unwary. The message comes to him across the top of the dike, a message that tells him of the swede field and the sorrel and weeds that choke the furrows. He is aware of the thistle seed scattered in the wind, and the nodding of ripened hard heads knocking on the stones, rustling gently and swaying; tall trees three feet high at a miniature forest's edge. Now he takes his time, sits and does nothing. Have you seen a countryman looking at the sun and clouds on a hill? This fawn and brown, long-lugs, as they call him, comes from the distant meadow and takes his time because he is soon going to bed. For him, like all things living, there is a sweet moment to be enjoyed between doing one thing and another, a moment that makes life what it is.

Standing where our hare is now, we might see those puffs of thistle seed sailing away into the heavens and feel the warmth of the morning sun. The dew has damped his flanks and dried from his fur. He sits with his forelegs stiff, his large, glass-marble eyes seeing everything from the flight of the crow to the wing-flicking butterfly on the stone, enjoying that last touch of warmth that is its Indian summer. The wood whispers, the first dead leaves tumble to the field and roll on the short grass.

Now, everything counted, noted and considered, the hare lopes down to the wood's edge. He hops the stones where the wall has tumbled and goes under the wire that tore wool from the sheep's back. He leaves no fur. The

damp mark of his print fades from the stone and he is in the wood. The
trees engulf him. You could not follow without making him run. He has
a dozen ways out of the wood, across the water and through the thorns,
over the wall, through the wall, down the tunnel of the bracken and
along the stream. The wood is quiet. He is a ghost in a ghostly place of
watery sunlight among the tall trees. His form is on the side of the hill.
Once someone dug a hole here, or perhaps a tree was uprooted and left
a hollow in the hillside. In the grass, screened by the ferns and bracken,
he has his resting place. He comes to it unobtrusively, silently, because
he has the stealth of the wild thing, the colouring of the wood wherever
he is. Stand above his form and look down. His long ears are on his
neck, his head on his forelegs and his back hunched. In a little while the
wood sighs and soothes him to sleep.

Look at the wood about this place. Look carefully, and see his way
of coming and going, his run. Unless you know about these things you

might imagine that an animal as big as a sheep made the run, or that it is the track of some small creature, a rabbit, a vole. The gamekeeper knows, the poacher knows. It is possible to look at the country round about and decide that rabbits are not running, for the rabbit makes multiple and forking runs, while the hare goes farther without breaking his trail. In the wood the hare only comes to sleep. He has no burrow, but depends on the shelter of the hill, the furrow, the dike, living above ground and in the sight of man. His colouring is no better than that of the rabbit, but the rabbit's territory is local and his hair is a shade darker or lighter with the season and place in which he lives, while the hare's fur or skin is camouflage in the ryegrass, the rushes, the brown earth and the brown wood. He is safe here just so long as some hunter does not spot the form in the grass, for then he may awaken to a dog's bark and fall to the roar of a twelve-bore. The wood has a system that protects the hare. The pigeon leaves with a clatter, the jay curses, the magpie chatters and shrieks, the squirrel makes his bouncy scolding from the high branches. The grass is threaded with crumbling cones, brittle sticks that warn the wood's population of man's coming. Even the pheasant leaves with a sharp call of alarm. Come down the wind and the hare will be away, so quietly, so stealthily that you will never dream he was there. Come up the wind and a pigeon will give the alert, a rabbit dart over the slope and past the hare's sleeping place. It is not that they all consciously depend on each other, but are part of the pattern of survival. Even when the pest killer comes with his gassing gear he never completely wipes out the rabbit. When the pigeon club sits in every wood to reduce the marauding flocks, pigeons come in hundreds a few days later. The hare that lives in the high wood lived a season ago in the low planting. Next summer he may race before a shot and carry a fatal pile of lead to some quiet dikeside where he will die. The magpies will come and help themselves to his eyes, the bluebottle will leave her eggs in his carcass. Another of his family will move from the low meadow to the wood, growing older and stronger on the uphill run. Perhaps the poacher's whippet will run this new hare to a lung-bursting death, perhaps the double woven snare will hold him fast on his early morning journey from the wood, or the net at the gate smother his struggles.

I remember going to the high wood day after day to rise a hare. The first two or three days I went with my gun cocked and my senses alert, but latterly I went just to see how easily he evaded me, how aware he was of my first movement towards his form. Day after day he was gone before I reached the place. Once I saw him rise a dozen feet before me and let him go. This continued until he grew tired of being disturbed and made his form elsewhere. I begin to wonder how it has come about that I like neither jugged hare nor roasted leveret. Once I could eat them with relish. Once when the old smoky-stocked gun came often to my shoulder, I disturbed the quietness of the high wood when it had that ethereal mist or evening shadow among its trees. Then I could eat hare, then there was more in seeing a bird fall than in admiring its powers of flight, but time changes more than one's appetite. What day was it that I left the kitchen when the hungry harvest crowd called for second plates of hare's-blood soup, hare not only out of season but a female hare more tender because she had been lately with young?

There was a time when the high wood was used as a sort of road. It was easier to breach the wall at either end and drive stock from one farm to the other than to make a long journey round when fields on either side were in crop. If cattle made full use of the wood and strayed in all directions, the dogs soon rounded them up, but oftener than cattle a sow was driven through. Although we bred bacon pigs, for a long time we had no boar. Our neighbours had a boar and he fathered most of our pigs. The sow was escorted to her nuptials through the high wood. No charges were ever made, but then, when rain threatened our neighbours' harvest, the threshing mill came or a plough broke, the favour was returned. Indeed, it was never remembered or considered as the return of a favour. It was part of life. This one gave his neighbour a much-needed broody hen, and the neighbour came to 'lay out' old so-and-so on the day he gave up the struggle, no matter how far in the past was the hatching of the eggs.

When the time came for the journey to our neighbours, a rope was tied on one of the sow's back legs and she was alternately urged with a twig and restrained with a pull as we proceeded, or, if she happened to be old, and less prone to running away, she was allowed to go untied and ungoaded, steered through the fields by the dog, who did no more than nip her heels in playful devilment. At the wood's end she was cornered while the dike was toppled to allow her to pass through. Once she was through, the dike was rebuilt and we went in search of our pig. The wall breaking and mending was repeated at the other end, and the sow allowed to go off to join her husband for a day or two. The older sows knew the way by heart. Their mating times were watched, but more than once, at feeding time, it was discovered that old Sorbie or young Skinflint had gone. Was she wallowing in the bog, up to her ears in the midden, or uprooting an acre of the cornfield? When such a thing happened it meant a search, a rapid search of all the creature's favourite haunts, every sty, every dark corner of the calf house, straw house and cartshed. All the gateways were inspected, for some of the most wayward sows could lift a gate off its pegs.

The first time I took part in such a search, I accompanied Willie. I had my first lesson in human weakness and cunning. Willie was not too bright. He was a great hand with a byre brush if it had a strong shaft on which he could lean. He invariably tipped himself into the midden with the dung barrow, or put his foot in a milking pail, but his aim in life was to show someone that he was no fool. Willie got down at the gate and sniffed, rose, ran a few paces and got down again. I followed. I was impressed. Here was a hunter, a discoverer of lost pigs. I knew the facts of life, but not the urge that compelled the breeding sow to climb the hill, cross the burn, wander through the wood, find a low spot in the drystone wall and fulfil her purpose in the scheme of breeding bacon. Willie was delighted with my credulity. No player ever put on a better show. The sow had deviated a few yards here, gone straight there for a spell, swerved again and turned uphill. This was amazing. Where could she be? Off we went into the twilight, through the gloom of the

wood. Willie could not see, but that wonderful nose directed us. We came to the neighbour's march wall at the far end of the wood, climbed the fallen stones and emerged on the rough road to the steading, greeted by a barking of dogs. The neighbours came out. It was late. What had brought us at this hour? Sorbie the sow? She was where she should be, in the boar's field, and soon she would be ready for home, a happy beast.

Willie and I went back with our news. I could not contain my admiration for Willie. The world had misjudged him, I decided. My aunts had put the word 'soft' before his name too often. He was a great tracker, hawk-eyed, a mighty hunter. In the kitchen, when I reached home, I expressed my delight at having seen Willie at work. Everyone had made him out a fool. Willie, who could track a pig a mile or two in the dark! There would have to be a readjusting of values, a fair credit where credit was due. My grandfather looked up, peering at me round the oil-lamp's tall globe.

'Just so,' he said soberly. 'Just so. Willie's the boy for that kind of thing. Now in the morning you'll watch him on the scent of the whin hoe he took away and lost, and after he's found that, we'll see his nose sorting the whereabouts of the turnip knife.'

Willie paused. The smile vanished from his ruddy face. He gaped at me in dismay and then scuttled for the loft stair. Someone explained to me very gently that a sow knew the way over a hill, and the thing that compelled the journey also made the rooster strut so proudly and cats cry at night. Willie never tracked another sow for me.

We are out of the high wood again, but let me take you back before we leave it once and for all. Let me take you to see the life of the owl and the magpie and how the cat was trapped by the keeper. When we have done, the wood will know us no more, and we shall be away when the sawmill comes to make an end of its haunting magic. If we need a pole for fishing, or pegs for snares, we can go to some other wood, but if we forget to look at the magpies and the owls, we have left this particular wood without seeing it as it is, for the magpies are as much the life of the wood as the sprouting bracken, the budding branches, the stream talking to itself among the stones.

Black and white, blue sheen, bright impudence, are the magpies, flirting their tails, bouncing and bobbing on the ground. Nothing on a canvas can do justice to them; no words describe them alive and in perfect condition. Their calls would have to be recorded because they are sounds both harsh and soft, the rattle of small seeds in a packet. You can walk the woodside and they rise from the edge of the trees and swing back and sail off overhead. You stand in concealment, waiting for pigeons, and the long-tailed, sharp-eyed magpie sees you there. Wary and cunning they are, gay and lively as the sea pie, the Oyster Catcher. Only when they are young and newly-fledged do they lack wits, but their wits are sharpened in a few days.

Yesterday morning, unable to sleep, I rose and saw them on the road outside my house. It was long before the milk float's morning run, hardly more than daybreak. They knew the world was asleep and the road was theirs as they toddled across it again and again. In the high wood all the long twisting strip of tree tops was theirs. Sometimes they left, sweeping across the field to pick at some dead creature or alight cautiously on the dike. See one, misfortune; see two, luck; see three . . . How the sayings

about magpies vary. Are they unlucky? Is it because they are scavengers
of the dead things? In some places the crow is considered unlucky. The
magpies of the high wood or the low wood were never unlucky to me.
They were beautiful and fascinating, bright and perky, like the jackdaw
that nests in one of our bedroom chimneys, despite my efforts to end his
days for him!

Watch the first pair nesting in the high wood and know that soon
the leaves will be thicker and the whole wood will seem filled with that
pillbox rattle, as though they had hatched a brood of thirty and not half
a dozen. The nesting pair come from a winter gathering. They nest in a
tall tree and bring earth from the field to plaster the twigs in the fork,
roots and fibres in which to lay their eggs. Sometimes the family is small,
sometimes large. In April, when the plover is nesting on the moss, the pies
are finishing their thorn roof. The thorn roof is there because they judge
the world by themselves, and take account of robbers. The way into this
thorny fortress is hard to find. The boy who swings and monkeys his way
into the high fork will have his hand torn by the thorns before he has the
eggs, those smallish blue-green eggs flecked with brown or grey.

Robbers and criminals every one, the gamekeeper will tell you, because
they eat the eggs of the pheasant, the partridge or the chicks of either.
They are robbers and pickers at exposed wounds on cattle and other
helpless creatures. When the young are hatched they sail to and fro,
heavily, short-winged, badly balanced they seem. They alight and lift
their long tails, hop down through the twigs, enter the fortress and come
away again. The gamekeeper looks for them in the tall trees, in the high
holly, in the big thorn, the hedgeside tree, wherever he sees that domed
nest. The pies look for the keeper too. Long, long ago, when game was
first preserved, a cunning began to develop in the magpie, as it had
grown in the crow and the rook those thousands of years ago, when the
first plot of ground was tilled. Now the magpies in the high wood know
the ways of man as well as the fox or the stoat. They are wary because
only by being wary does the carrion tribe survive. When the poisoned
bait is out not every fox eats and not every magpie dies.

The tawny owl and the cat, both crepuscular, both slit-eyed and silent, relentless hunters. The owl makes no more sound than the moth. He launches himself like a ghost from his perch, turns a wing to clear a branch and goes down the woodside. Unless you happen to look in that particular direction he goes unseen. His going and coming are unearthly. You turn and find him veering out over the field, brown and a blend with the night, soundless and so hard to see that it seems the night has opened and swallowed him. Sometimes he calls, but he is more of a silent creature than the nightjar purring on the bracken waste. He has the appearance of age, this brown wood owl, as he is called. He sits like an old man resting, top-heavy, about to topple from his perch, dozing and unwary, but he is not. He has all the light he wants in those almost shut eyes, at least by day. He hears as well as any bird. You come upon his roost to see him leaving. If he is forced into the open in daylight half the small birds go with him to make his life a hell. They are right to mob

him, for he is a great killer, an enemy of the wood as much as the hawk, more powerful, more ruthless than the rusty barn owl. This tree-stump of a bleary-eyed owl can slaughter the blackbird. He has eaten many a squirrel and has no fear of man when he thrusts a hand into his tree trunk nest.

The keeper has a way of making the tawny owl's life short. He provides him with perching places. The owl comes out across the little paddock where the pheasant chicks were being fed earlier in the day, and alights on the pole the keeper has erected for that very purpose. At the instant he alights the gin snaps shut on his legs. He topples, twisting and turning, looking at the starlit sky, knowing that he has made his last flight. In the morning, old slit-eyes meets his end. If he has not stiffened before the keeper comes, he feels the pole being lifted out of its hole and all at once he is in that eternal night.

In the tree his mate broods the white eggs and wonders why he has not brought her food. The light filters down to her. Her eyes close, she wheezes and sits in a sadness until night comes again. Whatever she finds serves as a meal. Quickly she returns to the eggs, scuffling and struggling down the black tunnel to them. Are they white because they are easier to see down there in the gloom? Certainly they are oval in shape because there is little danger of their falling or rolling over a ledge, but they are thick-shelled, for they are the eggs of a bird that is far from dainty about the feet. Indeed, the claws can deal with anything foolhardy enough to venture down to the nest.

The high wood shelters the tawny owl because he is part of the balance of life. It shelters the hunting cat to a lesser degree, for this cat is not the tuft-eared wild cat of the crags or the wild and remote forest, but the farm cat gone poaching and forgotten to come back to porridge and milk and table scraps. He is any colour from black to gold and white mottle. He has a name, this slinking hunter, but he has forgotten it. In winter he will return to the hayloft, a wild, lean beast, making a compromise with man because he has not quite the sharp cunning of the stoat, the speed and resource of the wildcat. The prey of the hunting cat is anything that crosses his path. He will lie in the nettles chewing away at the head and throat of a young rabbit. In the long grass he will make a debris of the feathers of a foolish bird. What a havoc there will be if he runs into the pheasant or partridge chicks! How pathetic is the squeal of the young rabbit; how helpless and tragic the last heart-bursting struggle of the small bird. It is a vast jungle, this wood at dusk and after dark. The hedgehog rolls himself into a ball and is safe, even when a dog is pawing him, but the vole, escaping the cat by a frenzied run along the dikeside, passes under the owl and the end is the same.

The life of the wood is preserved and maintained in natural balance, but for the pheasants to outnumber the stoats, owls and magpies and crows, the partridges to be plentiful in the root field, the keeper has to disturb the balance. He has to destroy the nests of the crows, blast the life out of the stoat and weasel, trap and poison and destroy. He watches the places where he knows the owl lives, he sees the signs that tell him of the fox, the badger and the foraging cat. In the high wood the fox and badger are absent, but the cat is there, furtive and wary. Walking the woodside the keeper glimpses him at noon, catches a flash of white, sees the abandoned kill and goes home for his gear.

Coming through the high wood one morning I discovered one of the gamekeeper's traps. It was a simple and yet an awful trap. The keeper had made a sort of lobster pot, a row of sticks driven into the ground and bent over to form a tunnel, and blocked at one end by pegs driven in to form a wall. The only means of entry was up the tunnel and over a gin. The sticks heaved and bulged, shook with the frenzied struggles of the cat which had entered to eat a piece of stinking fish. The dimensions of the trap were so neat that the cat could not get to the bait without crossing the gin. The walls were too close together to allow it to pass without being caught. There was no way out. The structure might have held a man down. I stood looking at the thing, wondering what made it shake, what animal was penned inside. Slowly I began to take it to pieces. As soon as the gin was sprung the cat snaked out and streaked for the bracken. Perhaps the keeper set up his trap again. I did not go

back to see, but I am sure he did not catch that cat a second time by the same means. Probably he put down a poisoned bait.

It grows colder. The leaves are flying from the thorn tree and the stubble is getting old. There is no life in the high wood and the stoat will soon be in his white. We can go to the wood at the tail of the loch to see the duck and the big bog hare. Look across the country and see the neat cornstacks in the stackyards, the hard appearance of the river, and the way the hedges have become thin. There is a shiver on the land after noon, and the brightness in the west is brief. The geese are due out of the north and the old man, his blood thin, remembers the winter he saw the snow bunting in his garden, pink and beautiful, but so numerous that the superstitious shook their heads.

Can you ride an old ramshackle bicycle, carry a sack containing a gun broken down to stock, fore-end and barrels? Can you wobble through mud-stained puddles in the old road and put your foot on the ground to make a brake at the road-end gate, and on all the hills on our way? The countryside is half asleep already. Yonder the ploughman is leading in his team. The gulls have gone from the furrow. The ploughman's cheeks are red with cold, his hands chapped with the bite of the wind. As we pass the farm by the road someone peers at us from an open-fronted outhouse, pondering our destination and our business. What have we in our sacks, what-like folks are we at all? A servant girl with tomorrow's kindling in her arms stops and stares, turning her head full round, letting the wind blow her hair across her face. It is no use resenting this impudent stare, for they are taking note of us as one of the events of the day. 'Two men on bikes with sacks on their backs went past a while ago. A wild-looking pair they were. I know the cut of them.' For this, I must apologise. They know the cut of you, my friend, because you are in my company, and I have never been particular to go to the woods in immaculate riding breeches. They know my cut because I kept company so long with others who prefer the woodside to the fireside; who know better the call of the jay than the barkeeper's goodnight.

We are off on the long road past the Doon wood, the croft among the whins, the stony fields where the sheep still graze, and through the village where the cottage doors are snugly closed, and the scent of peat smoke lingers in the grey stone street. It is cold, so cold that the publican's dog is no longer on the flags at the door, and the bantams are huddling under the henhouse. Winter breathes on the meadows and the bog fields. We are going through a black-earthed plain where the ling grows in summer, where all the trees lean away from the prevailing wind and there is neither curlew nor small bird in the gorse. Look at the sky. It is clear, and deep as a great pool. In two or three hours it will contain all the stars of November's sky. Soon we will be at our destination, among the willows and gnarled, deformed old trees that grow in water-logged, sour ground. We go past the holding with its fresh whitewash and its red-painted iron roof. A dog barks and an ancient turns slowly and watches us go. He is old enough to have been in the ruins of the deserted village in the days of 'the battering in', when, if you listen to legend, their neighbours came to put an end to a feud by battering in the doors and slaughtering their enemies. Wave to him and he stiffly lifts his arm in greeting, a little self-consciously, perhaps, wondering, 'Now who were they? A pair of poachers by the look of them!'

We are not going to poach. We are going this long way to see the duck come in over the willows, to see them alight on the pools and feed. We are going for the pleasure of crossing that hill by the winding road, and seeing the glint of the water away yonder among the trees; to see the heron beating out of the waste on its way to roost. The heron has had his day after fish and frogs, stilt-walking through the waterholes, striding in search of the unwary water vole. As he comes he is followed by others that make a harsh cry and go slowly, heavily away, leaden-coloured, leaden in their movements.

This is the track to the wood. Throw the old bicycle into the thorn thicket. When we return we can extricate it. Hurry, for the light is the light of late afternoon, and the duck will soon be on the move. Watch where you go among the trees. Don't go through the gap between the sallows. In that place, six months ago, a bullock lost its life. The oozing bog will swallow you to the thighs in a second and away in this place your calls for help would do no more than frighten a bird or two. The moorhen and the coot have left their footprints on the mud among the reeds. Here, too, winter is crawling through the woods. The leaves have gone from brown to yellow, fallen, and covered the water, and then slowly drifted away. See the downy feathers at the water's edge, a sort of tideline made by the breeze. Duck were here this morning. An hour ago the heron walked this water and a trout was speared in the shallows. A pair of snipe leave the black marsh. The bird that sprang into the air from firmer ground was the woodcock. He has been there among the dead leaves, making his borings for worms, absorbed in his feeding, soundless, a blend with the browns and fawn-mottle about him, but bright-eyed, sharp and very wary. Like the snipe, he is a fastidious eater. His flavour is delicate, his flesh white on this account.

Our moment has arrived. The duck are over. Somewhere behind us three or four are stretching their legs on the bank and now, before us, the drake sweeps in over the trees. He seems to misjudge his distance, because we can hear the splash of his landing, see the hurried flapping of his wings. Now he is turning about and the ducks come down to his side. They do not feed at once. Five more cross above us and the last of the formation deserts and shoots his neck out as he drops to the water.

All are alert. It is still day, and so long as it is day a fowler may come stealing through the trees. They are safe from almost everything else while they are out there. Nothing can take them unawares but the long-barrelled duck gun poked through the branches. They swim in a little cluster, doing a sort of waltz, during which some of them are looking in all directions and listening for your boot being sucked by the mud as you move on a yard. Now they are half satisfied that the world is as it was at dawn, and yesterday in the gloaming. One ventures into the rushes, another sucks at something below the surface. Stay where you are. One movement now and they will all be in the air, their wings whirring and whistling, the drake making his escape with water dripping from his feet as he rises.

Did you hear the call of the moorhen? Dusk among the reeds and rushes. Have I brought you here for nothing? We haven't shot a duck and the day is gone. We haven't seen the hare, and the hare too is safe. Two birds are fluttering and splashing after each other twenty yards from you. You could shoot them, but you would drown trying to recover them. We must come back tomorrow and bring Mick's water dog. We must come at dawn, and when the birds are gone we can move to the harder ground among the trees, and rise the tall bog hare. Was it not enough to see the duck sweep in over the trees, to see them black against the sky? An artist can capture the sight, but he cannot paint the wind through the trees, the sound of their wings, the magic of twilight in sound and scent. There is surely nothing more beautiful than to see duck flying in the moonlight or the light of rising day. When the sun is up they are away, up on the loch, roosting afloat in a pack, snoring with heads twisted round on their backs, swinging at their moorings as the surface of the water is pressed down and then released by the wind. Take a boat and row out to them and beauty is gone, as though you had thrown a boulder into a trout pool.

Back we go, with all the care that a man needs to keep himself upright, undrowned, free from the clutches of the marsh. There is just a bow of a moon. It does no more than make a glimmer above the blackness of the trees, but its fleeting light glints on a pool. Turn aside and walk away from this place. Stand still. The bit of a moon comes sailing out of the darkness, a candle carried by some sure-footed, hurrying witch. It makes us stand still again, for the light falls through the twisted arms of the trees, shows the water and the blackness of the boggy ground, and we are lost for a while, so that every step has the hesitation of a marooned cat. Why did we come here? Why did we stay so long? What is the magic of the wood and the bubbling, whispering water among the reeds and rushes? We came to see the birds, we came to loiter among the trees and see the last streaks of day. Now they are all gone. We are in the blackness of night, for the clouds have swallowed the moon and we can see nothing. How many miles away is the barking dog, in which direction the beast that lows? The cold water swims over our boot heads, our feet sink into the black earth. An endless age passes before we are back on the track. Something calls in the night, a little tinkling sound, some passing flock of sand birds up there in the night, and then the curlew calling to his nearest neighbour.

We are going back home, with the guns once more in the sacks. The faulty lamps light a stretch of road and then leave one or the other of us in darkness, just when we fear we are near the deep drain. It begins to rain, and no bird flies, no creature calls. The wind tugs at our clothes and makes us long for the shelter of the wood; not the wood of the bog we have come from, but the wood of the blanketing firs, the warm wood that filters the gale from a fierce, desperate thing to a little wind. What a bare desert of a place the world would be without its woods and trees. How long would man live once he had broken the balance, as he has so often set about doing when his need for timber seemed to be greater than his need to survive? Here, four or five trees shelter a farmhouse. He knows the value of these trees. That line makes a windbreak and allows him to grow oats or wheat. When he cuts down the planting, the copse, the old oak wood, it takes him a little while to see that the drainage is different, that the soil is washing into the hollow, and new crops of rock are in his field. The lumbermen come and haul away the timber and every yard of the fields on either side changes in nature, new weeds, new grasses, more sun, less humus, water-logged drains in wet weather, overflowing ditches. A year or two, and the man sees what he has done, but how long must he wait to see it as it once was? A tree, the tallest, sky-brushing pine, cannot be grown in a day. The oaks he slaughtered, as so many greedy people have slaughtered them in Wales this year or two past, cannot be grown in two weeks. They took as long to grow as the oldest man in the village; they were maturing when his grandfather was a boy, but it is no crime to destroy what you cannot replace! It is a crime not to turn the oak woods into cash, and everything is put right when a spruce is planted where the oak grew.

We are off our road. We were going home, through the howling wind, between the hawthorn hedges and the hills of swishing, swaying gorse. How your heart leaps when a wind-battered gorse bush suddenly springs up from the top of the drystone wall, a looming black ghost in a dark grey sky! How welcome is the oil-lamp's light in the window, the smell of the kitchen, with the peat of a thousand-year-old forest burning in the range, the kettle singing and the cats clustering in the hearth.

Wake up. Wake up. No, it is not day, nor is the house on fire. We are going back to the wood at the loch's end, back to the water birds flighting in the mist. Get out of bed and come with me, for we are calling to take Mick's water dog from his cottage garden, and this time perhaps you will come home with a duck or two, the fawn mallard or the little teal, or both. Perhaps you will have a hare in your sack, a boot full of water, or one leg black with the bog, like a black thigh-stocking. We have a long way to go. Can you ride and lead a dog on a bit of binder twine, or manage two sacks instead of one? The water of the pump is cold, but we have no time to relight the range fire. Plunder the dresser, take flour-dusty scones from the meal ark, the cold meat of the fowl we left at supper. Oh, this is no time to be fastidious, you are impatient to be among the trees, to see day coming and put up a gun for your dinner.

Mick's dog must come without its master's permission. We must ask him another day. The dog shivers and then smells the guns. He knows where we are going and runs on his twine lead like the well-trained beast he is. He has short hair, a sort of Labrador look, a whippet look. The look he has is on every poacher's dog from here to the other end of the country. If we abandon him or he abandons us, he will be home before night. Forget the jinking lamps. It's as well that we ride in the dark, for we can go unobserved.

You can see no more than the colour of your palm. The light is ghostly over there among the trees. The water looks grey. It has shadows upon it. They might be duck, might be moorhen or coot, or just the strangeness of the light. Take the twine from the dog's neck and bid him come quietly through the trees. The duck are going to and fro across the wood higher up. How many are on the move? The teal are with us, see how they twist and turn in flight. They are small, the smallest duck, but what beauty is on the drake. Here they come, down in a breathtaking dive, swerving up, turning and coming in again. Get ready. You came for this moment and you must have it. It is enough for me to watch. The sound of your gun is muffled. The morning is folded about us. The echoes are lost in the wood. You have one down in the pool and another over there among the rushes. Send Mick's dog. He splashes across the pool and brings the first and then off he goes for the second.

Do you see the beauty now? Do you see speckles on his breast, the streaked head and his guinea fowl back? Does it not make you a little sad to have stopped this water bird in all the splendour of its flight? They are nice enough out of the pot and perhaps it would have taken you a lifetime to discover the colouring in its detail without shooting one. The dog brings you the duck. What a poor broken little thing she is. All the duck from here to the loch are flying now, speeding up and down in the mist.

In a little while the day will come over the hill and the duck will be away on the water, safe. Let us look for the hare across the stream where the sagging plank spans its course. Be careful or you will be off in the flood. Up on the higher ground the trees are thinly spread. The old dead grass, grass that was waist-high in the summer, gives shelter for the hare. He can evade us round the trees, cross the bare patches and escape into the next thicket before we have a glimpse of him. It hardly matters. Stand still for a while and one will bob out of the grass and present himself to the cooking pot. You have had enough. The bills of your duck are hanging out of your sack. The moorhen is rasping among the rushes down there and the snipe are flashing away over the trees. Let us go while it is still safe to be on the road.

We saw no sign of the deer. They were there, somewhere, away among the trees, so deep in the waste that once the gunshot had sounded we had no hope of ever seeing them. Soon, when the cold wind blows and there is no food to be had, they will be out of the wood. A grey morning will find them on the hill where the turnips grew. Here and there two or three turnips that have escaped the carter will still be growing on the headland furrow and the deer will have them. They will be down where the roots and kale were scattered for the wintering sheep. When we look across the hills we will stare for a minute, wondering if we are seeing

right. Deer on the pasture, two, three, four, brown, white-marked, alert.
Two strides across the first field, and something will give them warning.
Off they will go, faster out of the pasture than the snipe from the bog,
springing up, across the dike, over the hawthorns, away, bounding so
swiftly that it is hard to believe they were ever there at all. Away up in
the hills, where the mist winds round the crags and there is nothing but
the wind and a scree of stones, you might lie with glasses and watch the
behaviour of the red deer, but when they are down in the forest moor,
raiding the farms, they are hard to see. A man believes they have been in
his fields when he knows their tracks, sees the havoc they have wrought.
He wishes for a rifle but he has too much to do to think of any way of
preventing the raid.

All the country is one field to the deer. They sail over the fences, the
hedges, the walls of stones. One or two minutes and they are at the back
of the far wood, half an hour and they are beyond the rugged skyline.
Somewhere, away in a lonely place above the moor, among the boulders,
they will halt and look back, their sensitive nostrils will sniff the breeze;
they will listen, watch and walk on, like nervous gentlewomen. Nothing
could come near them but a bullet from a rifle.

Yesterday on the road out of the village I came across a hedgehog
walking from one side to the other. He had been disturbed from his
winter quarters, it seemed. I fancy a dog had discovered him, or perhaps
he had grown hungry. It was a dangerous little adventure, this crossing
of the road, for twice cars passed and twice he rolled himself into a ball.
I picked him up and put him in the hedge bottom, for I have a soft spot
for the little hedge pig. Once, a long time ago, I had two tame hedgehogs.
I had them for a season. The autumn wore on and they vanished to find
somewhere more to their liking than the range ash-hole.

Of all the creatures I had as pets the hedgehogs provided me with
the greatest pleasure. I enjoyed rearing them, because, in a way, I was
responsible for them. When the kitchen emptied after the midday meal
I used to call out the dog and make for the woods. One day it would be
the high wood, another day the low planting, another, any of a dozen

woods within walking distance. Once in the wood we had a sort of understanding, the dog and I. If I became too absorbed in the behaviour of a small bird, or he wanted to snuffle at a burrow and fan the air with his tail, we went our ways alone and met later. On the day I acquired my hedgehogs we went to a wood along the top of a hill. It was a wood filled with ridges and banks, short burrows through which rabbits played hide and seek. The dog became interested in one of the burrows. I stood for a while, staring up into the trees and then wandered on. The light brown earth sped from the dog's scratching paws. This was the way he wanted to spend this particular afternoon, and he was enjoying

himself. I wanted another glimpse of a chiffchaff that was flying about in the high branches. I came to the end of the wood, stood again peering up, then turned and wandered slowly back. How risky it is to behave in this way, for in the grass a broken branch may catch one's toe or a foot may stumble into a rabbit hole. Many times I almost fell, but at length I came back to the dog. He was hot in his mining. A great mound of earth lay behind him. He was head down in the hole. I could see that he had found some kind of nest. It wasn't the nest of a rabbit, for the doe would have gone into the open field to have her young. Out of the hole came grass, a great ball of hay, leaves and fibres. He had discovered the hedgehog's litter. I drove him off with a stick and fumbled in the dead grass. Five little hedgehogs, smaller than my fist, lay curled in the bed. There was little hope for them now, for the litter had no protection. The bank had gone from above them. I searched the grass but could not find the mother. She evidently slept elsewhere. At dusk she would come back to her litter and find this awful devastation.

It was a warm afternoon but by night the air might be chilly. I did not know what to do. The little hedgehogs were soft-quilled. They were not afraid, and after only a second or two would uncurl and allow their little black snouts to be stroked. I held one on my palm and watched its beady eyes almost lost in the black and grey hair of its head. They would hardly be welcome at home, but I decided to remake the nest as best I could, using a slab of stone as a cover, making a convenient entry hole and putting three of the five back. If their mother came back she might find some new place to shelter them, but at least two would be safe with me, if they would eat porridge and milk, or table scraps. I put one in each pocket of my jacket and set off for home.

So I came by Hubert and Herbert, the little pigs of the wood. They liked porridge. They thrived on milk, bustling to the saucer to rob the cats, and although the cats spat and slashed at them with their paws, the hedgehogs were always successful. Their activity was at night. Through the day they dozed, for they are creatures of the half-light, stealing out of a hole when the bat is flying, hunting when the owl hunts. At evening, when there was gloom in the kitchen and everyone was off to bed, the hedgehogs scuttled and rasped across the tiled floor. They grew bigger, more plump and wonderfully tame. The dog had great respect for them. When he came near to sniff they rolled into a ball, relaxing when he went back to his sleeping place beneath the form. As the days grew colder they were oftener in the hearth. When the ashcan was withdrawn they crawled into the hole to sleep. They were never prevented from going out, but they seemed to prefer the house. The instinct of the wild was strong, however, and a day came when they disappeared. They had gone off to seek a place to hibernate, some hole which they would fill with dead leaves, some quiet, dry lodging in which they could go into that torpor of winter sleep. They did not come back. I imagine that when they awoke, if they did not die in the unfamiliar coldness of the earth, they had forgotten that they had once fed at a plate and allowed their black noses to be stroked.

They probably forgot that they had ever been called such foolish names as Hubert and Herbert.

The hedgehog likes a dry place. It thrives where there is insect life, where it can grub and root like the wild pig it is, but it knows that some animals have a way of making it unroll, so it comes out only at twilight. Once we had a collie that dealt with a hedgehog by carrying it or rolling it to a waterhole, immersing it and biting at its vitals when it unrolled. Often I have seen country boys using one as a football; what awful injuries the creature suffered I can only imagine. The two I kept were clean little animals, although I was told later that they were exceptional, and that most are infested with fleas.

Before we leave this countryside, I want you to come with me to the woods we saw from the top of the hill, the smithy wood, the wood at the edge of the peat moss, the wood beyond the crofts, the wood above the bog. Watch the cormorants crossing from one bay to the other; follow their line of flight until you see that wood in the distance, the wood by the sea, where the wealth of a big estate has put down laurels, rhododendrons, deodars, cypress, cedar, yew and other trees foreign to the countryside, but beautiful as the Chinese pheasants that walk the rides.

First to the wood above the bog, because, like the low planting, it is a place for the longnet. It is a narrow wood, no more than a windbreak of trees; a few hundred firs, an ash or two and a dozen beech trees. Come with me at dawn so that you will know your way about it in the dark when the net is being set up. The wood above the bog is a conspicuous place. It is the nesting place of a few pairs of pigeons, a wren, a finch and a mistle thrush. It is safe to be there when the world is half asleep, or when darkness blankets the bog and the fields about it, but it is as well not to shoot here at midday. The people round about can see you up among the trees and watch your going down the bare slopes on either side. Daybreak is the time. There is mist in the hollow, clinging to the thorn hedge, hanging above the burn. The way to the wood is along the

hedge, through the barbed wire apron of the march fence and up the hill. This hill has been pasture as long as anyone can remember. It is poor ground. The turf has grown so thick that it has choked itself and made a dead mat through which thin, feathery grass grows. Here and there you will see little patches of green, nibbled short by the sheep, but it is a fawn hill all the year. Its only colour comes when the thistles bloom or the vetch is in flower in the old cart ruts that cross its brow.

Tread softly, for there are stones buried among the grass and the sound of your boot on a stone would make an echo up in the trees. A pigeon or two leave and a cock pheasant rackets away across the country. No, this is no pheasant wood. He was a passenger on his way to some new shelter. When we crossed the fence he was on the hill. The sound of our coming made him run, arrowing up through the grass, fast into the wood with his head down and his tail sweeping, then lifting as he prepared to launch himself. He stopped running, walked with nervously-lifted feet, his head raised, his red-marked eye and ringed neck still for an instant, and then he was away, warning the world with his alarm note. Yonder he drops into the dew-drenched kale field, a clumsy, wing-flapping bird like the cock of the farmyard.

We have the wood to ourselves and there is nothing to be seen, nothing for the blind man who sees no life sign in the mounds of red, freshly-disturbed earth, the marks of scurrying feet that tell of a great rabbit colony. You cannot get to these rabbits with a gun, for they are gone before you reach the wood. The slopes could be snared, but the yield would be small. On the far side the hill flattens at the wood's edge, making a shelf of ten or fifteen yards where a net can be run out. Put down the gun. You might easily knock over the hare bobbing in the grass below us, but on the road over there a man is wheeling a cycle up a hill on his way to a farm which we can see beyond the hedge. Tonight you will have all the sport you want and come home with a great bag obtained without a crashing echo round all the hills about us.

Hold your tongue. It is dark, but in the lulls, when the wind has done shaking the trees, a voice carries a long way across the fields. The rabbits are down the hill. They will come up fast enough once the dog is sent about his work; they will come in a great wave, bounding and bouncing to our net. Put your hand to the setting of the net and work quickly. This is the wonder of a wood on a cloudy night, when the wind rises and falls and the dead beech leaves rustle. The moon comes tumbling out of the sky and glints on the tops of the trees, picks out the gable of a farmhouse, not white but grey, and rolls back into the enveloping clouds once more. The ground is hard and the pins are not easily set up, but, after all, the business of setting up a longnet would be nothing if all went well. A rabbit rushes across our feet. A pity, because in a few minutes the net would have blocked his path. Tomorrow he will be one of the few on this side of the trees when the sun comes up. He will hop out over the old turf and wonder what happened in the night.

The dog is off on his circuit of the field, down to the ditch, along the hedge and back across the slopes, working closer. The rabbits are on the move, tumbling into the net, bagging themselves in its slack folds, making the whole thing alive with their struggles. The line tightens. Come quickly because we have a great haul, enough to make the sacks too heavy before we reach home. The dog has lost his head with excitement and is barking with all his power. Hurry, for you never know who is out at night.

You have worked hard. Whatever they say, it is not a lazy, hands-in-pockets way of earning a shilling. It takes patience, care and much effort to get a bag with a longnet. It will be a season before it is worthwhile coming back to the wood above the bog. In the morning the message will be there for the sharp-eyed, the message of the little round holes evenly spaced along the woodside, the white belly-fur of the catch, the flattened grass where we knelt to bundle up our gear. Look at the wood in the light of day and see the sunlight behind the thin screen of trees, the silhouette of the fir tops, the tracery of beech branches. Nothing exciting or romantic about the place, just a few trees along a hill, a hill like a sleeping sheep.

The wood beyond the crofts is tall. The trees stand above the knolls of gorse and bracken. The kestrel sails above the trees and a sparrowhawk comes down the hollow, making a score of small birds fly ahead in a cloud of terror. I went to this place a long time ago, when trees were much taller, much greater in diameter; about the time when the bone-handled pocket knives in the ironmonger's window were my heart's desire. I went to look at the nest of the kestrel. A year before, a pair of crows had this nest, but the kestrels had come to the wood and taken over the old nest, high in an oak tree. The only way to see the nest was from an adjoining pine. This tree had been a lookout post for the sons of a crofter for many years. The way into its top branches was easy. The first fifteen or twenty feet were scaled by putting hands and feet to six-inch nails which had been driven into the trunk. Once in the top of

this great tree, so strong and alive, swaying above all the others in the wood, it was possible to overlook the country round about, to see the marsh where the curlew nested, the thickets sprinkled with blackthorn blossom.

The kestrels had four eggs when I first looked into the nest. The birds kept away while I was in the pine, but as soon as I climbed down, the hen went back to her rusty brown eggs. When the young hatched, the hen flew out of the tree as I climbed the pine and alighted in another tree a little way from me. Often I thought she might come sailing in to attack me, but she left me unmolested. The young were being fed mice and insects. They were a hungry brood, and as they grew the parents went to and fro by the hour, sailing over the moss and the bracken, spotting their prey and swooping down on it. What eyesight, what effortless flight from one hovering place to the next. I came back to the wood one day to find them all gone. The young had flown. A week later and they were mewing in the little planting, venturing over the shorn hayfield after the shrew.

In the wood beyond the crofts I carved snare pegs and pins for fishing lines and climbed almost every tree.

The smithy wood attracted me from the day I first went to the blacksmith with a horse in need of a set of shoes. It was a wood almost exclusively of firs, tall, straight firs, towering over an undergrowth of nettles and dwarf blackberry bushes. A great rookery was the main feature of the smithy wood. The nettles were splashed white beneath the rooks' nesting places, the blackberries and grass laid flat by a great number of fallen twigs. The wood was always full of the cawing and quarrelling of the birds and the sound of a stream. The stream ran out of a dam used to provide water for driving the smith's waterwheel. Long ago a fir had fallen into the dam. Two or three branches supported the tree, making a sort of bridge, and it was possible to climb out along the trunk and fish the dam which contained some great eels and a few trout. Once, in the manner of Huckleberry Finn, I reclined on the tree trunk and threaded my line between my toes. Nothing happened to disturb me. I gazed into the wood and chewed a stalk of grass. Somewhere in the dam a large eel became hungry and wriggled his way to my dangled worm. He took the bait and the hook completely. The line seared my toes. I almost fell into the water. The surface of the dam boiled with the eel's struggles. He was a great brown beauty. My line was strong but I could do nothing. It was impossible to thread my way back along the tree, managing the line and watching what I was doing at the same time. At length I gave up and cut the line. I think I was a little afraid of the eel. The cut end of line snaked over the dam and vanished. The eel went back to the rocky bottom to digest the worm and cope with the hook. He may be there to this day, as thick as a man's wrist, one of those great eels that have never been able to complete their life journey, from the sea to the river and the little stream, and back again to the sea.

The blacksmith was always ready to lend me fishing tackle when I visited the smithy. The wood gave me shelter from those who passed on the road. I could fish the water unobserved and many a small trout I took below the dam. One day, with a larch pole and a bit of brown line and a few worms, I caught thirty-two trout, all big enough to be eaten. I have seen fly fishermen proudly display half a dozen much smaller fish. Oh for the wood by the dam again, and those naive trout that never looked twice at a bait!

Have you ever been to a peat moss or seen the business of making the ancient forest into fuel? Every year we went to the peat moss to cut and set up peat. Once all the moss had been a great wood, stretching back up the slope to the west, sheltering all the country from the gales from the sea. Woods had grown and died, been replanted, or had self-seeded and grown again. How many decades, how many layers of wood make a great peat moss where only the water level stops man digging deeper? In places there seemed to be no end to the peat. Part of the moss was bounded by fir woods, woods that surrounded a mansion and its lattice-windowed lodge. The lodge slept in the trees behind two large white-painted gates. Across the drive sat two or three chicken houses and the fowls roosted in the wood, picked their way about the slopes, safe, for in all this wild country the fox and badger were unknown. Only when the estates were broken up, gamekeepers died out, and preserves became timber reservoirs, did the fox come back. It was one of my great delights to go to the wood on the moss, for the dikes round the moss were old, the trees brown and shady, the air . . . the air of the peat moss, the scents of the peat bog, of heather and ling and crackling gorse.

The days of wealth, the days of the landlord snug in his country estate were numbered for a long time, but he died hard, the country squire; abandoned his possession piecemeal in the circumstances of higher costs of upkeep and repairs. Today he has lost his voice as well as his possessions. When I was small I went often to the peat moss and the woods were unravaged, but later, when I came back on holidays from school, I discovered that the sawmill was in at the side of the trees, away on the fringe, it is true, but there, nevertheless, a symbol for the owner who was trying to pay his way. A month or two and the lumbermen were through the first stand of trees and the clouds were visible behind the second. Like a cropping beast, the tree-killing machine came on.

There is a great activity about a wood camp, a screaming of circular saws, the gusty life of the steam engine, the rattle and clang of chain tackle as horses drag the trees out of the wood. All this goes on in the resinous air, among the heaps of sawdust and the churned mould that bogs the struggling horses. Chips of pine fly, handsaws rasp, and a man with a climbing belt and iron shins to top of a tall tree, cutting away

the branches. Almost before he is on the ground, others begin axing the tree or working the crosscut in a steady rhythm. The bluebell shoots are mashed in a pulp, the unborn anemones are ground into the earth, the primroses destroyed. Oh, the sad march of the axe and saw, much more dangerous and deadly than the fungus, the boring beetle or the burning lime of the starling's roost. Here, away in the side of the moor, where the grouse fly in packs and the stunted blaeberry bushes grow, progress, necessity, the left hand or the right hand of a banker's ledger, are having their way. In winter a searing wind comes down from the skyline, driving rain and shifting mist. The urgent movement of the lumbermen is no more. A few wooden huts are shivering in a hollow, old yellow chips lie about the place. In the spring the bracken will rise to cover the scars, a rabbit or two merge from the bank and begin to breed, but the tall trees will not grow again; the passing pigeon will fly on.

This thing happened to the wood on the moss, happened quietly, the way a thing can happen in a remote place. I remember cycling up the grey road – a sort of greenness about the road's centre made it plain that it was no oftener used than it had been – and seeing the engine at work, hearing the crash of a falling tree, seeing the blanket-shirted crew about the work of execution.

I went home and remarked, 'I see the sawmill is in the wood on the moss road.'

The kitchen was busy at the time. No one heard my remark. The same necessity was driving farming, the cheapness of bacon in Denmark, the price of eggs in China. Yet, it was all no more than a rabbit's nibble at the timber of the country. It took a war to put the woods down. Who was it that went about England putting down acorns that made the Navy? When we have a plastic material to take the place of wood, someone may be quixotic enough to go about putting down acorns so that our great-great-grandchildren may see what an oak tree looks like.

A little farther along the moss road, across a humpy hill or two and past a roadside cottage, stood the trees of another estate, the sacred trees, the trees around the home farm and the mansion. Here were gullies walled with ivy and woodbine, with sycamores thrusting up towards heaven, deformed ash and twisted oak, green with a pastel shade on their trunks and limbs as though some wood spirit had been among them with a paint pot. In the drive, winding away above a stream, yews and cypress trees swayed and cast their showers of water on the pebbles. Here grew cedars and deodars and foolish monkey trees dying as they grew. Such neatness and order in everything, from the iron fences to the trimmed grass. To walk here was to be transported into some strange foreign world, to smell the cedar, to touch the sticky round cones of the deodar, to see the exotic birds. Yes, here even the birds were different. Little Indian ducks on a pool, peacocks in all their splendour, the golden pheasant, the magnificence of China, all so well protected in the seclusion of the beautiful grounds where there was such a hushed stillness that a country boy's heart beat faster. Here the magpie hardly dared to chatter in case the keeper was at hand, the jay did not laugh. There was a sacred stillness broken once in a while by the dainty feet of a hunter trotting along the gravel, or the dignified purr of a car gliding down to the lodge gates. What woods, what fruit, what colour of birds, and the yew berries fallen on the short-cropped turf. Not the wild woods where we might poach, but a sort of a sanctuary for the lovely things that money brought from abroad, things like the peach tree and the grape vine, the orchids and the melon plant. Such places are vanishing from the country and we have lost something – something not to be found at Kew or the hideousness of the Zoo, and those who have never seen such things will never know their loss. Perhaps they are blessed in that alone.

I've lived long enough in the Welsh village I'm living in at the moment to be recognised, if not as a native, then as a man of this place, not a foreigner. I've been here long enough to have been poaching in company with men of the village and to have found my way about the hills and valleys and far-back woods. The woods of Wales are subtly different from the woods of Scotland or England. The hills are closer together, the woods fill the hollows, woods of Welsh oak, hazel, willow, blackthorn and chestnut. I have often escaped my immediate worries by making off for the woods before dusk. Sometimes I took an old single-barrelled gun with me, and sometimes I carried nothing. In a strange place everything has the fascination of newness, of being unexpected. A step through a new wood is slower because there are new things to see. No two trees grow in the same way; the topography is different. In these woods one stands often in a hollow looking up to the sky on either side. A rabbit appears up there, no more than thirty or forty yards away, and hops along on the background of the sky itself, a fox speeds along a ridge, a pheasant appears, turns and vanishes again and the pigeons come in right above one's head.

On my first walk through the woods behind the village I met another man with a gun. He stood in the shelter of a tree waiting for a rabbit to come out. He was a pot-hunter, and what better excuse for lounging in a wood?

'Thought you was the owner of the place,' he grinned.

I smiled too. I looked too much like a tramp to have been mistaken for the owner of the old gun I was carrying, let alone the wood in which I stood! We joined forces. In an hour we were away across the hills, looking down into a little village at the bottom of a steep slope, peering at it through the trees growing uphill, straight like an army on parade. It was autumn, sunny autumn, and the smoke from the village chimneys drifted up to us.

'Couldn't shoot here,' my companion remarked. 'Wake the whole place up.'

I felt that way too. It wasn't that anyone would have started up that heart-breaking slope after us, it was just that the evening, the sunlight, the smoke above the village were too peaceful to be disturbed for a pigeon.

'I never like to shoot them when they're cooing,' he remarked of the pigeons. A Welsh poet.

A man can't take poetry home for his dinner. On the way back we crossed a wheat stubble. I shot a hare, my companion shot one too. The lane took us on a long detour past a country alehouse. In we went. The poet sold his hare and bought a pint of ale. He grinned at me again. 'I'll have to go out in the morning now,' he said, 'but, man, was I dry!'

He began to sing after a while, David of the White Rock. I knew I was at home. Before we parted we arranged to meet again. For a while I could hardly go out in the village without meeting my new acquaintances, for when I met one, I met another and another. The driver of the grocer's van would pull in and hail me.

'I was at Ty Mawr yesterday, just at the corner. There were three pheasants on the field. I stopped the ole van and got out the ole gun. I was all set when who do you think came riding up . . .'

Endless hours, endless talk, moments lived and re-lived in the woods and hills. An invitation to poach, an invitation to go out with a ferret, a longnet, to go fishing, to help shoot a fox.

'Saw you Saturday. Eight pigeons you had, wasn't it?'

This is the way of a man's good name. I began to consider my good name. I lost my friends, slowly, one by one. Dick, who drove me to the station in a taxi the other day, turned round and smiled.

'Remember the day we had diggin' out the ferret?'

I remembered.

In Wales I came to know new birds, the spotted flycatcher, the yellow wagtail, the grey wagtail, the green woodpecker, the lesser spotted woodpecker, the little owl. I saw the buzzard and heard the little owl more often. I came to know old Brock and the fox, and gathered the fruit of the bullace tree.

Up the valley, in the scrub wood beside the lake, I watched the spotted flycatchers for the first time, and in the same place I discovered the shy little spotted woodpecker, a black and white miniature of the green woodpecker, old yaffle that flies across my garden and perches on the telegraph pole; that goes laughing through the trees of the glen, pitching himself across the field in long loops. The thing about Wales is the smallness of its fields, the oldness of its villages and farms. How long have the tenacious hill folk clung to their stony acres? In the hedges, far away in the quiet valleys, one comes across gooseberry bushes, ancient bushes that mark a place where a cottage once stood. Sure enough, within a few yards one finds the broken walls, the crumbled foundations of houses that stood long before George Borrow tramped through. In the woods behind the village I know two apple trees, a damson tree and a sweet chestnut all growing within a short distance of a place that once was some Welshman's home, a place fenced in with thorns, oaks and blackberry tangles higher than a man.

On a bright September morning, when poaching was still strong in me, I went with a friend to the back of beyond, carrying a gun, a few cartridges, and some bread and cheese in a knapsack. We trudged uphill and down, we scouted woods, blundered through gullies and over ridges. How far we went only our boots knew. Our eyes were always on some new wood, some clump of holly, some undergrowth that might shelter

a new bird or animal. We did not once fire our guns, but a gun to some men is like a pipe to others. It is not always in use. Before dark we came to an old walled place among the trees. Here, among the walls, were other trees, trees laden down with fruit, bullace trees. On either side in the hedges were bullace trees, and the fruit was large and ripe. We ate a few. They were sweet, as big as damsons. The crop was so heavy that the limbs were breaking with it. We might have picked a hundredweight and left two hundredweight more, but we filled our knapsacks and carried them home. The fruit bottled well enough. The autumn went and in midwinter the first jar was opened. How sour they turned out to be! What was wrong? Was it the magic of an autumn day? We had many bottles. They were all the same, as sour as sloes. I never considered it worthwhile going again to that faraway place to bring back the bullace tree's crop. The sweetness of the fruit that day had something to do with the mellow light of September, the fresh breeze across the bracken, the sun going back behind the mountains, the dog barking down in the valley, the clatter of our boots on the road.

Although I do not venture with the gun now, every autumn I go out to gather the harvest I discovered on my poaching expeditions. On a hill there stands a wood in which grow the finest, largest mushrooms. Those who see them are afraid to lift them, for the scarlet-marked fly agaric grows among them and Death's Angel not so far away. The beech tree, the spruce, the oak, all seem to have their own funguses. The honey agaric grows on the little fir and the fir dies, a growth foretells the end of the birch. At the fringe of the wood the toadstools stand in the long grass, even among the nettles the mushrooms grow. The place has only to be sheltered a little, to be away from the wind, to have just a little sun to generate the heat in the mould and decaying leaves, a warmth that would make the snake lay her eggs, and the fungus growth springs up almost overnight. The colours are as wonderful as the colours on any bird: fawn, creamy white, brown, dark brown, liver-shaded, blue-tinged, crimson and orange. All these shades in places where the ground is dun, the grass blue-green and old, the nettles pale and weak; shadow in its own place, behind the hedge, away from the light, damp, yet with the warm breath of life rising from its very roots and fibres. In the autumn I know the mushroom from the agaric. I have been tempted to try a dish of puffballs, but my family seem a little reluctant to cook them for me. I find it hard to persuade anyone that toadstools are not all fatal poisons!

Before the mushrooms, the blackberries. It always amuses me to see townsfolk picking away at two or three straggling bushes at the roadside when a few yards away are bushes heavy with fruit. But the townsman is notoriously blind, and the countryman is reputed to have a habit of walking in the path of London buses! After the blackberries, the hazelnuts and elderberries. Have you had elderberries in a pie or dried them to use as currants?

Up the hollow stood a wood that had been planted by prisoners in the 1914 war. Prisoners in the Second World War helped to cut it down. The first crop after the trees had gone was a magnificent display of foxglove. Where had they all come from? Had the seed been lying dormant in the wood? Every foot of the wood was covered with the foxgloves. The following year half as many grew. Today no foxglove grows there at all, but a few untidy bushes are taking its place, a spindly beech is thickening out into a fine tree, gorse and broom are spreading, covering the broken branches and the close-cut tree stumps. The pheasants have come back. There is enough cover now, and through the gully the stream floods once in a while, enlarging the boggy patch, making the willows shoot, the rushes grow taller. Buried in the dead grass a few logs are still to be found. Going up the hollow on summer evenings, I have often encountered an old man with a fir pole on his back, a pole he has salvaged from its decay in the grass, a pole to provide heat in his cottage in the winter or stop Pentre Isa's sheep breaking through into his garden . . . I have a vision of myself coming down the same treacherous gully in the dark, carrying a hare, a gun, a bag full of mushrooms and a log on my back, slipping and sliding, growing more determined at every step to see the load reach home, most of all the hare and the mushrooms, but only a little less the firewood. I have never been able to explain the great satisfaction I have always had in bringing home such an assortment, but how comfortable I felt, recovering before the fire, my gun put away, the hare hung in the larder, the mushrooms being prepared in the kitchen.

Could any shopkeeper sell me this thing, with his brown paper bag and his kind offer to have it all sent up?

I have never grown tired of going to the woods. I hope I never shall, for then, I am sure, old age will have me.

Do you know the way of a badger? Have you been near enough to him to see his shambling gait, his grizzled coat, that stern-high way he ambles up the hedgeside in the half-light? I became acquainted with Brock here in Wales. I knew him well before I had ever seen him. His work after wasp grubs nearly lost me the sight of an eye and I met two men who testified to the badger's will to live with a story that made me swear to help protect him, no matter what was said against him.

Brock lives less than a mile from my house, but I imagine his relatives are much nearer. Two or three years ago young badgers were reared in a hole beside the bowling green, another was killed crossing the main road. Go up into the woods, and unless you know about badgers, unless you can read the signs, you might think every hole was a large rabbit hole or the lair of a fox. The badger is more nocturnal than the fox. He comes out in the gloom, makes his rounds and is back again before daybreak. He doesn't exist for those who don't see him. He is a friend to the bee-keeper, destroying the wasps. He is a grubber among the roots, a gatherer of grass and hay for his bed, old splay foot with the striped face. The farmer loses a chicken and blames the fox or the badger. One I met attributed the loss of every bird he had to the badger, and yet, somehow, I felt he was wrong. A fox has the heart for wanton slaughter, but not, surely, the badger? He has cunning, a great sense of smell. He will starve himself to an awful skeleton rather than come out and be caught in a gin trap. Those who know him say he will stay underground and die rather than let himself be taken, but send down a terrier, a stout-hearted, yapping little Border terrier, and old Brock will give him the fight of his life. Most of his time he will be below ground. In winter he will be in that half-hibernation, in summer he will be waiting for the darkness so that he can travel his path in the night. He trundles along, from one soiling scrape to the next, turning off, guided by his scent to the grubs he is seeking, turning back again when the wasp nest is a raked-out shambles, and all the juicy grubs are eaten.

You will hardly ever catch him above ground by day. The story of his being caught out in broad daylight reflects no credit on man. It had been warm, a warm, drowsy night and a warm morning, with the sun beating down on the gorse. The badger had wandered too far in the night, perhaps. At all events, he was sleeping in the thick gorse, lulled by the heavy scents of summer, when two men came hunting for rabbits. They were putting a terrier through the gorse when the terrier met up with the badger. He did not run, but backed away a few yards, snapped, moved on, snapped again. He came to the edge of the gorse patch. The dog yelped and the men with guns turned and saw him. They were wild, heartless characters, these two. One lumbered forward and threw up his gun, blasting the badger and putting him down. The stricken beast slowly rose and staggered into the next clump of gorse. The killers followed, their dog dashed ahead. The badger was forced out. A second charge went into his side. He began to walk on, a blind, helpless creature, mortally wounded. The harrying terrier was mauled for his pains, the men with guns followed up. Another shot, another, and poor Brock's entrails dragged behind him. The cost in cartridges was too high. They could not afford to finish their awful work. The badger crawled on and died at the mouth of his earth. When the men came past that way they collected part of his skin to show what barbarians they were.

He deserves to be left alone, in peace, but one evening I passed a place where two men were digging. They had terriers, picks and shovels. The brown earth was piled on either side. With great delight they delved in the earth to bring the badger out. The following morning they were back at the place; the following evening they gave up. The hole was more than twelve feet deep. The badger had been digging his way ahead of them perhaps, but they could not match him, and the particular terriers had not the courage to fight him, wherever he was in the bowels of the ground.

If he takes a chicken once in a while, I ask that he should be excused. He has a right to be looked after. He is a gallant old codger.

I admire Brock for his determination, his will to live, and I admire the fox for the same thing, although he does not stay to fight, using his cunning to keep alive. I was coming out of the wood a year or two ago when I met a farmer who was fuming over the cunning of the fox. It seemed that chickens had been going faster by the fox than the black market, and their owner had set a trap. It was a good trap, a proved method of getting a fox, and in the morning there he was, caught as surely as a fox was ever caught. The farmer approached his hencoops – they were set along the shelter of the trees. He could tell from the hysterical cackling of the birds that the fox was trapped. There was no need to cock his gun. He put the gun down against the side of one of the coops and went to the trap. The fox was dead – but let the man tell his story as he told it to me.

'He wass dead. I put my foot on the trap an' lifted him out. New dead, he wass, and warm. I laid him on the bank and set the spring of the trap again. When I looked up he wass off! Off like the very wind, he wass. Never looked back! My gun was round the corner. Foxin' he wass! Foxin'! Next time I take a dead fox out of a trap I'm goin' to kill him just to make sure. Them birds wass worth the best part of twenty pound, man!'

A fox should be able to laugh, like a hyena.

The first time I met a fox face to face I was carrying a load of firewood. It was growing dusk. He stood not twenty feet away and looked at me. 'So this is the old red fox,' I thought. Whatever the red one thought, he regarded me with all the impudence of a collie dog. I put down my load of sticks, not knowing what I was going to do. Perhaps I had it in my mind to approach him, but he would have none of it. If I hadn't been close to a fox before, he had seen man and knew his ways. He turned and loped away across the field, up the slope to the copse, pausing once to look back at me. I saw the farmer shortly after, but could I say that I had seen a fox? In addition to my kindling I carried a shotgun and what excuse could I make for not having blown the red one off his feet? Lack of wits, perhaps, for he had stood long enough. I held my tongue. It was enough to gladden my heart, and still is, the memory of the fox,

standing there at the edge of the thicket, looking back at me with one paw raised, and his sharp face full of the devil.

My second encounter with the fox was on a bright autumn day. He went slowly up the hedgeside and trotted through a partridge covey. The rising of the birds made him halt and stare, but he had been well fed the night before, or drugged with the sunshine and soft breeze, for he made no effort to stalk them. He looked across the field. I was standing beneath a tree. He saw me and went unhurriedly on, through a fence, up a hill and into a wood, his brush trailing behind him. I began to search for the home of this fox. I saw him often about this place before I located his lair, and when I did I was surprised that I had been so blind. It was under the trunk of a fallen tree. The day had been cold, a leaden day that suits the bareness of the countryside before Christmas. I was through the thicket, past the pool and the place where I had thought to put up a woodcock, when I came upon the first feathers. They were the feathers of a goose. Stories by the thousand tell of the fox stealing a goose, but I doubt whether he often gets the chance of getting away with such a large bird. I followed the trail and there was the goose. The fox had had a fine orgy, in the sagging undergrowth. Parts of the goose were everywhere, the chewed head, the tip of a wing and feathers by the hundred. It was plain that after the feast he had crawled in to bed. A day later I went back. From the position of the debris he had been out again to feed. What a happy Christmas, what wrath on the adjoining farm! Probably the farmer and his wife put their heads together and laid a poisoned fowl for him later in the year. All at once the tracks to the lair under the tree faded and grew old. I knew that he had gone the way of all his kind, no matter how cunning.

Across the gully I discovered another, a dog fox with a home in a hole near a birch tree. Twice he came up out of the gully within a few yards of me and I felt tempted to shoot him, but each time he fascinated me so much that I only remembered my duty to the farmer after the fox had gone. I was too interested in an animal that was new to me. I had not grown up with the fox.

To most of the hardy farmers round about the fox is a menace to be dealt with ruthlessly. One I know has a fox in a glass case which he uses as a scarecrow. The results are achieved, as far as I can observe, in rather an odd way. The birds do not seem to be afraid of this stuffed fox. They mob the glass case. Perhaps while they are doing that they are not eating the wheat. The first time I came across the novel scarecrow I noticed the glass of the case was broken. Reynard stood on a moth-eaten mound, staring across the brown harrowed field with bright beady eyes. His hair was falling out. Poor beast, he had the mange and had lost his proud place in the parlour.

Yesterday I heard of a party of fox-killers out over the hills behind the village, killing more than a dozen in a day by the use of dogs, picks and shovels and guns. The balance will soon be restored. The rabbits will have to be gassed and ferreted, and while the pestologists – what a word for a catcher of rats and moles! – are after the rabbits, the foxes will increase. Perhaps, like an old molecatcher I knew, they will make sure they leave just one or two to maintain a supply for next year!

Although in these Welsh woods I have come to know the fox well, I have only once shot one. I feel virtuous about that. Fox-hunters might shake me by the hand if they thought I had spared the fox so that they might run him to death, but I care nothing for fox-hunters. I did shoot a fox one warm summer evening. I had been out through the wood on some idle journey. I forget whether it was to watch the nest of the nuthatch, that mud-stopped hole in the dying tree, or the secretive treecreeper, searching the trunk for insects, hooking them out with his little, daintily curved beak. I found myself on a larch-coned path down through the trees. There was no undergrowth and I could see ahead for a long way. On the floor of the wood something moved. I did not hurry, but began to watch. I watched a fox in a gin. He was held by the back leg, brutally held at the end of a chain fastened to a piece of wood. How far he had dragged it I do not know, but he had twisted and turned to free himself until his coat was impregnated with pine and fir needles. He turned and looked at me, a glassy-eyed stare. He was past caring about man. His leg was skinned, red and raw, the bone showed. The torment must have been all he could bear. It was too late to give him his freedom, for he had no life left to enjoy. I wondered how long he had been there, dragging his burden about the silent wood, suffering alone, blunting his fangs on the iron of the gin. He began to twist and thrash again. I had not been watching long, a minute, two minutes. I lifted the gun and aimed at his head and put him out of the world of chicken baits, gin traps and searing agony. It was a close shot, a very quick end to his suffering. The wood echoed with its sound and I took the trap from his leg and took it home with me. Whoever put it down would have to find another. I hoped he would get his wrist in its jaws, as I once did.

We have been to woods that are gone and to the woods that are there still, along the valleys of Wales. I might have taken you to see the nest of the wryneck in the wood in southern England, to find the nest of the turtle dove, that small dove that purrs on a hot afternoon, but perhaps you are sore of foot, stiff-necked from staring into the tree tops, weary of the long trudge to bring back a few mushrooms or a bag of crab apples. Most of my woods are gone, the woods of friendly trees, the ferny banks, the heavy scented hawthorns I knew when I was a small boy. I never failed to count them when I left home. The last thing I looked at was the top of the high wood peeping over the turnip hill and the little wood along the hollow. When a bend in the road put these out of sight what more was there to see? The tops of the pines in the garden, towering the old apple trees and, away to my left, the woods on the river, the wood on the stream, the smithy wood standing around the dam, the woods on the far moss, sentinels to the peat bog and the nesting place of all the moor birds.

To return from school was a journey of anticipation until the train came down through the hills and halted a brief moment at the station. I could stand in the cool air of daybreak and hear the rooks in the elms. Once I heard that sound I was home. Minutes or hours could pass in peace when the sun came up and showed me the woods I knew so well. Back in the hills were woods through which I had travelled with a relative, selling

cattle food to the pinch-penny hill farmers who lived up among the fir
spikes, along the marshy shelves, where the hour was told by the crowing
of the moor cock or the height of the sun above the distant sea.

I confess to having taken you on this journey that I might enjoy myself,
going back down through the sunrise on a single-track railway with a
fussy locomotive and long plume of smoke on my way to the woods I
once knew, to the hazel copse near the Devil's Elbow and the creamery
wood, reflecting in the mud banks and the water of the river. What a
sound as the milk floats beat down through the trees with their cargoes
of jangling cans; what a painful beauty to be seen crossing the spans of
the bridge and going uphill with the pony's head low between the shafts.
There was no urgency, no need for this journey to end.

We have done no more than visit these places. There are other woods,
fresh woods, woods in which I will stand tomorrow and the day after.
There are always fresh woods, little corners of the countryside where
the bird and the animal kingdom hold sway, places where we can hear
the dawn chorus, or the last little twitter before the birds sleep and the
badger ventures on his round. Brush the moss from your jacket and
throw away your whittled stick. What company you have been in! What
an idle time-waster you have been these past few days! Haste you away
across the field, back home with your bag of hazelnuts, your elderberries,
your excuses for being where you have been.

PASTURES NEW

IT IS A COMFORTING THING that where the countryside's wealth is in its soil, for the growing of crops and the raising of cattle, the landscape does not change. Stand at the door of the most modern farm in such a setting and you will see the hills and meadows as they were hundreds of years ago. Here and there a new fence may have been put up, the way into a field altered, or a Dutch barn may take the place of the old stone building, but the contour of the land remains as it was. If the field you look upon fed good fat sheep a hundred years ago it is likely that it will do so again. This book is called *Pastures New*, new because I hope to bring them to you as they were in the morning of my life, but old too, as my grandfather saw them, and his people before him. In the main it is the story of a place I love, as it was when my eyes were wide and wondering and the plover's nest on the spring furrow the most beautiful thing in the world. Let me take you through these fields, give you their story and their life, as old as the oldest stone in the wall, as fresh as the hawthorn seedling newly sprung on the bank of the stream.

The townsman names his streets and avenues, his rookeries of flats, his forests of suburban homes. His mental place is in the buildings he has erected, and perhaps he sees beauty there. He must be happy, because he remains in his acres of brick and mortar most of his life. The countryman names his fields or discovers that his ancestors did it for him. The wood has a name, the path has a name and the hill too gets a name, and often they are descriptive of the land, its shape, its crop, its size.

The names of the home fields were all utility ones, giving indication of their locality. Long ago they probably had Gaelic names, but if they had, the names were forgotten. When my grandfather farmed them they got new ones. The field that held the old stackyard and the elms became the Sow's Field. It was given to the pigs, for its crop was stones, mushrooms in autumn and little yellow lilies when the year was young. The Wee Field was behind the house, a sort of sacred field that was never ploughed. It belonged to the hens and the pony. The Switchback Hill ran back from the Big Hill. On the Switchback a lazy man could lie in the sun and let the summer take care of the weeds, for no one could see him here. There was the old road field, the bog field, the Wee Five Acre, Clutag Hill, the hill away from the morning sun, the March Gate Field and the Far Hill, or the Low Planting Hill. They marched such places as the Other Clutag Moss and the Malzie Hill, and looked on the Barlae Hill, that always had a horse grazing its steep slope, and the distant hills of Grouse, where the geese were on the green turf and countless sheep bleated through the spring. When these places were as much in my heart as the air of the high hills was in my blood, I wandered the fields, and though noon was warm and a thousand rooks went over before dusk, my days were mostly morning when the light was on the branches of the pines in the garden and hens were cackling in the cartshed.

I found my first partridge's nest in the Wee Five Acre, I caught an eel in the water that ran under the bog field, shot a pheasant on the Big Hill, fished a trout from the burn in the Wee Field and stalked a hare on Clutag Hill. How many times did the march pool flow over my boot heads! I saw these fields in root and grain and gathered mushrooms from their ancient turf. I walked them in the silence of daybreak and stumbled through them when night obscured the whitewashed walls of home. Somewhere in the peace of early summer I heard the yellowhammer's song. I must have been very young when first I heard it, but the sweetness and sadness of it impressed themselves upon me so that I am again a child when I hear it now, just as I am at home when I hear the curlew's cry. Once I forked every sheaf of a harvest from the stubble to the cart, and oh, the days I toiled at haymaking, the potatoes I lifted when the digger was scattering the black earth!

When about the business of writing a novel it is my habit to go now and then and sit on a rock that overlooks the hills and fields behind the village where I live. There is no pleasure greater than the contemplation

of a countryside, a countryside at work, about the tasks of the day. The pattern of life seems set out before me and the little pattern of my own thought takes better shape when I have the perspective of man and the place in which he lives. When I was a small child I was fortunate in living in a place that had rolling country about it, round hills and flat meadows, farms stretching away into the distance and places with names that were poetry in themselves. When I was three the Big Hill was in corn. How can I remember such a thing? That year an extra seat was fitted on the binder so that I could sit beside my grandfather and go to and fro across the Big Hill as the corn was cut. Down there, across the Wee Field's greenest of grass, the kitchen chimney put up its peat reek to the morning sun, and a tiny figure, one of my aunts, went off through the march gate to catch the baker's van at the road-end – the morning of my life. When the sun was halfway to noon someone struggled up the hill with tea cans and a great basket of scones and jam-spread pancakes. To lean against a stook of corn and drink tea from a blue-banded bowl, as I have done hundreds of times, is greater delight than the finest dinner at any city eating place. There is a first impression of everything, if one can only recall the time and the impression together. I remember the

Big Hill at harvest, so long ago. I remember that year because I heard the music of the melodeon and the brogue of the Irishmen who helped harvest the corn. I have a score of later memories of the Big Hill, but of the Wee Field, the field behind the house? Here, surely the first thing I did was to chase wild bees with a wide-necked bottle filled with clover heads and sugar. I used to trap as many as I could, bumblebees, brown bees, bees with red sterns, large and small, furry and fascinating, until I fumbled my corking and got stung. I can still recall the clover sweetness, the powerful scent of the confined blossom. Many a day I ran myself out of breath and lay panting on the grass of the little field, watching my quarry rising into the summer sky and growing smaller and smaller as it sped away.

The Wee Field was my playground. It had everything a child could desire, round hillocks of gorse, gentle slopes, a drystone wall, a thorn hedge, a burn with peaty banks, places where laying-away hens nested, waterholes where the ducks left their eggs. Here the wagtail pinned his nest above the burn and here were the holes of the water vole. In this place I watched the breeze make a speeding ship of a curling white feather, and here too I toppled into the mud and came out like a black man, yelling for my mother. When I discovered the secrets of setting a snare, it was here I set my first, watched by my grandmother. Grandmother believed in encouraging a child in its play. She went to the harvest field where a rabbit had been killed by the binder, brought back the carcass and put it in my snare. I was not to be deceived, however. I knew my rabbit had been killed by a binder knife. No amount of praise made me satisfied that I had caught my dinner. I was born country-wise.

Have you had a meal of plover eggs? A long time ago they were a delicacy on the tables of fashionable London hotels, these brown, green and fawn marbled eggs. Dozens found their way there and when the year was young in the north, in the last days of March and early April, the country boys went in search of them, boys from the age of five to fifty, for a man who can wander the fields all day in search of the nest of a bird is a boy at heart. By the nature of things – work while the hours of daylight lasted, six days a week – Sunday was the day for egg lifting. On Sunday there was a holy quietness. The good farmers went off in their traps to church, the dutiful sons rode home from their places of work to visit their aged parents, the farms slept. Those whose blood responded to the invigorating air of early spring put their caps on their heads and went off to the ploughed fields or the pasture to wander about, observe the birds and find the nests. Come with me as I often went when the peewits were flighting and calling across the fields.

Sunday morning and the spring cart gone with its load of churns. Breakfast over for those who have found time to eat it. Half the family fed and the other half hastening about their Sunday duties, anticipating their afternoon nap, those looked-forward-to hours of rest. It is Sunday and more than Sunday, the first in April. Fields are ploughed. Tomorrow the corn sacks will be along the headlands and men with the art of scattering seed will be walking to and fro hand-sowing the oats. Put your cap on your head and call the dog. It is cold across the fields, put a scarf round your neck and make sure that your boots are comfortable. We are ready, with our snack in our pocket and all of a bright day before us. The little field behind the house wets our feet with its dewy grass, a startled rabbit goes bouncing off to the warren above the ditch. The sounds are the sounds of spring and the morning as light-hearted as the bird singing on the tip of the tall gorse. On the hill the peewits are calling, half of them in the air and half of them along the furrows. Study the beauty of this bird, the contrast of black and white, the jauntiness of his tuft and the madness of his flights. His note is spring itself. The peewit nests not only on the ploughed land and the pasture. He nests in the rough and on the moss. Beyond the moss another field, a field of sheep, a hill of young grass half-grown, half bald, a ploughed field, a wood and another moss. We can walk until the day is old, walk with the sunrise, come back with our weak shadows before us when the cows are lowing and dogs are barking.

Halfway up the first hill we see a pair of birds running the furrow. The cock bird rises and sweeps in over our heads. His call is urgent. The black and white of his feathers is all we see, for our eyes are quickly on the ground. We cross the furrow and come back. The air is filled with the cries of a dozen pairs of birds. In this field we might find four dozen eggs or we might find one. The peewit has a habit of making false nests or depressions on the ground. They are hardly nests, for they are no more than the form of the hen's breast in the earth. Country lads call them 'cock' nests, but from the false nest or the real one neither bird ever rises. They run and rise twenty yards away. While we are walking to the field the birds are moving. When we are on the ploughing they are rising with cries designed to attract us as far from the eggs as possible. The first nest is right before you. One more step and your foot would have crushed the eggs. Look at them. Are they not wonderful? Four eggs as near a blend with the ground as could be. They are pointed and, like the egg of the curlew, large for the size of the bird that laid them. Turn these eggs so that their points are outwards, leave the place and return, and you will see that the hen has carefully turned them point-inwards again. They are made this way so that they will not roll away. The hen sits comfortably on them until they hatch and as soon as the chicks are

out they can look after themselves; at least, they can run and crouch on the earth and blend with the ground about them so well that until they move they are invisible. The birds of the ground have this protection. It is part of the great pattern of survival. A restless pigeon chick would fall to his death had he the leg-power of a ground bird, but he hatches a helpless creature, top-heavy, hardly able to move an inch. When time has taught him the dangers of his world he is almost ready to fly. Walk past the moorhen's pool and the sooty chick that was born yesterday will scurry from the nest and paddle into the over-hang of the bank.

The peewit seems all black and white when he is twisting and turning about our heads, and yet if you could see the hen on the nest, she is not so much black, not so much white. The white is hidden beneath, the back has shades of grey and brown, a sheen of the earth itself. The eggs have a stationary camouflage, the chicks a general colouring that suits whatever soil they hide upon. The eggs of a pair nesting on the furrows will be a shade near to the soil, the eggs of those nesting on the moss will have olive-green predominating to such an extent that you may think we have found the eggs of a different bird. We have found what we came for. We may find a score more. Tomorrow the man who sows the crop may crush a clutch or two. By the end of the week the harrows will break up the last furrow and the cries of the plover will have sadness in them. Pick them up. It is sad, but so is the death of a lamb to provide your dinner and it is more brutal to breed a fowl so that you may systematically rob it of its eggs. We have come to walk the fields and moss and get a few fresh peewit eggs for supper or for breakfast. Walk on. The thing happened before you were born and it will surely happen after you are gone.

Tom, who worked for us, was the most clever gatherer of eggs I have ever known. He had an eye for a nesting place, even on ground he had never crossed before. If a curlew rose from the moss, he looked about, indicating the probable locality of the nest with a wave of his hand. If the bird had not a nest within twenty yards of the place, it had no nest at all. You might quarter the ground without finding it once Tom had made his prediction, if Tom had made a mistake. Spring got in Tom's blood. He watched the peewits, the curlews and the oyster-catchers that often made nests on the field. Later he watched the partridges and pheasants with equal success. He made many a shilling delivering the eggs of the latter to the keeper. One Sunday he went off across the moss as soon as his breakfast was done. He was gone for several hours and returned looking miserable. On the course of his travels he had encountered a family of boys on the same business. They had demanded his eggs and chased him for them. Tom had fought as well as he could but they had overcome him. He was wearing the eggs when I met him, for they had beaten him on the head and his cap had been full of eggs. They had trickled from his hair and ran about his ears. On the following Sunday, when he went off again, he was accompanied by the dog and carried a useful-looking stick.

The peewit is about the pasture and makes his call in spring and early summer. As the days go past he gradually disappears. The growing oats shelter the crake. The partridge calls at evening, but the peewit is away on the estuary. Before he comes back his brother, the golden plover, will be on the grassland, tinkling and swirling in rapid flight. Stalk them with a gun, and they are as much an epicure's dish as the peewit's egg. They rise and alight again within a few yards of their resting place. Fire a shot into them as they fly or when they are settled and you will lift four or five. It is strange how naive these little birds are. Perhaps they come from some distant, silent beach, some smooth stretch of sand that never bears the mark of a man's foot. The peewit is gone and roosts and feeds in the estuary, on the meadows where the grass is coarse and the running tide makes the ditch fill twice a day. In autumn a flock or two may come across the pasture, but it will be spring before they are back to their nesting places, back in the brightness of the spring sunlight.

Now the afternoon is growing old. There is a chill wind over the moss. We have our dish of peewit eggs and turn home. The moss pools are cold, the light hard and wintry as day begins to fade. Before we have clambered over the march wall the milking will have started, the pigs fed and the hens gone to their perches. Lay your eggs in the bowl. Look at them again, at their symmetry and colouring. They are part of the beauty of spring, something of the brilliance of a spring day, something of the awakening earth. When they are fried they are rich, the yolks almost orange, the whites crisp and thick. There is nothing quite so tasty. The eggs of the curlew are harder to find, and, I think, a little stronger in flavour. Enjoy them. You walked half a score of miles to find them. A long time ago, when I had a sudden fancy to taste plover eggs again, I wrote to a cousin who farmed in the north and he made a Sunday walk and gathered me a dozen. The box came by post. I scrambled to cut the string, but, alas, the eggs were broken. I could only stand with the fragments of shell in my hands and remember the days of my childhood when I walked those same acres in search of the peewit's nest. I was downcast and yet there was a certain nostalgic pleasure in receiving the package. I looked at it again. It was tied with binder twine, a hastily made parcel, something from the far moss. The cry of the birds sounded in my ears as I looked at it. I smiled as I remembered Tom with the rich yolk hardened on his face.

The plover is a protected bird. The taking of its eggs is forbidden. In places where it was once plentiful it is now scarce, not so much owing to the countryman developing a great taste for the eggs, I fancy, as to the methods of cultivating. Many a ploughman following his horses would spot a nest before he reached it and move the eggs from the path of danger. Often a man with a set of harrows would do the same thing; but a man on a tractor looks behind half the time and the eggs and young are often destroyed by the wide-ranging cultivator. Some years ago a large number of migrating peewits were swept out into the Atlantic in a gale. So many perished, I am told, that the numbers left to nest were seriously reduced. Where they are plentiful they are a delightful sight. On Anglesey they never seem to be scarce. I imagine that in the fenlands they are just as numerous. I have not been back to the place where I spent my childhood for many years. I wonder, do they still run the furrows there as once they did? In twenty square yards I have often found seven or eight clutches.

When a man had work on the far side of the Switchback Hill, or down in the bog, he was out of sight of the steading. Time was the climbing of the sun, the movement of shadows and, now and then, the signs of dinner being ready on other farms, where the hoeing boys left the turnips or the haymakers came out of the meadow. When neighbours were out of sight, away, perhaps, on their own back hills, there was no way in which a workman could guess the time but by the sun. The grasshopper sings as well at noon as he does at one and two. Often, when the heat has radiated in the earth and baked the soil beneath the turf, his song is happier when noon is long gone. Few of the men we ever had owned watches, fewer still had reliable watches. When the wind was right, it was possible to hear one of two whistles, the creamery whistle and the train whistle. If the wind was from the west, these whistles went unheard. Grandfather would come out into the court and look at the shoulder of the Switchback, or the old road field which led to the bog, feel in his waistcoat pocket for a whistle and stand and blow it until his breath was short. The note of that whistle, blown by the strongest lungs on the place, was often lost. It had a long way to go, across the Wee Field, the stackyard, over the hawthorns and the ash, across the clover, the rustling oats, up out of the hollow to the gorse and the drystone wall. The sound had to travel like the light-hearted butterfly, away on

the scented breeze of summer. The man on the back hill only knew his
hunger, the perspiration in his shirt, the tang of the swedes, the drowsy
perfume of the whin and the broom, the ryegrass sward freshly laid by
the blade of his scythe. Often he plodded on, along his furrow or the
path of the scythe's stroke. Time, after all, is nothing but the length
of a shadow, the strength of a reflection in a pool. When this thing
happened on the Switchback Hill, the family took their midday meal
without concern for old Tam on the back hill. They grumbled a bit
about his deafness, at his stupidity in not seeing somehow that it was
past noon and the hens had retreated from the court to the shadows of
the gig house and cartshed.

The Switchback Hill could do this kind of thing to the industrious and
the lazy. The sun of the morning and the sun of early afternoon beat on
its farthest brow. Across the hollow was Barlae wood; away beyond,
Barlae Hill; up the hollow, just a glimpse of a neighbour's steading, a
grey stone house with narrow windows, and a sleepy look about it,
morning, noon and evening. Many an hour have I spent on this brow,
working with the light hay crop, stooking corn. On Sunday mornings I
liked to go there and lie on my back so that I could face the sun when

everything was at peace. Our laziest byre boy loved to be sent there to
work, for he no sooner reached the place than he threw himself down
and promptly went to sleep. Morning would go quickly and noon soon
pass. In the kitchen at home, when the meal was over, my aunts would

argue as to which of them should go to the faraway place to bring old
Tam to his senses. Once the decision had been made, the aunt who
accepted the duty would hurry off, up the old road, through the old
road gate, across the burn, on and on between the gorse hedge, through
the tall milk thistles and the sorrel beds to the 'slap', the poled gap in the
dike. If, by some unfortunate chance, old Tam had come to his senses
and started home without warning, he met one of the daughters of the
house on this rough road to the Switchback and bowed his head under
the abuse.

'Have you no sense, Tam? Couldn't you see it was long past twelve?
Did you not hear Father blowing his whistle for you? What were you
doing? Sleeping at the dike side? Just you wait until you get there. The
Man with the Whiskers is waiting for you!'

The Man with the Whiskers was grandfather. He was spoken of by
his daughters in this way without disrespect and without humour. Later,
when he was ageing, they often added the word 'old' before 'man'. It
was another term of respect. When the workman who had stayed away
came in for his meal he was asked about his sense of time.

'Didn't you see the train smoke? Did you not hear the creamery
whistle? God sake man, it's nearly three!'

Time on the Switchback Hill was the same as time in the bog, cutting
round rushes for thatch, the flight of a small bird from a thistle head
to the stones of the dike, the movement of a 'spider' on the surface of
a waterhole. Along one side of this hill ran a rough track which had a
foundation of broken stone. This track was a continuation of the old
road, but it led nowhere. The place that had stood at the end of this
track was long since crumbled. Somewhere in the stones of the wall
there may have been the stones of an ancient farmstead, or a village. I
liked to think of the black brow of the Switchback sheltering a village,
a sleepy clachan in the sun. Oh, it was the place for it, looking at the
day. In the hedge beside the track was a magnificent rowan tree. The
blackberry bushes grew among the stone-heaps, short, strong bushes
that bore the largest, juiciest fruit. All this place needed was an ancient

village to put up its smoke. Instead, the hill sheltered the hare and was hunted by the stoat, for the light grass was the home of many a shrew and vole. Once, on the slope above the march dike I shot two magpies that had been dining on the eyes of a freshly killed hare. I remember feeling a little sorry about this, for the magpies looked as ugly as the hare when they were dead and I had restored nothing with my gun.

It was hard to hear the noon whistle in the bog and on the Switchback, but from most other places it was possible to quickly reach a piece of rising ground that allowed one to see the farm buildings. This fact had advantages. The shirking youths could climb a hill and get warning of their master's approach. They could see if the afternoon or morning tea had left the steading and whether the dog had been sent round the milkers.

Willie, whose stomach was as good as any watch, although, like a watch, it sometimes gained a little, was in the habit of spying the land more often than grandfather liked. He had gone to look for his tea as usual when the old man arrived over the brow of Willie's chosen hillock.

'Have I not told you before to keep at your work? Isn't that what you are paid for?' grandfather demanded.

'Ah, but,' said Willie, 'I wasn't lookin' for my tea this time.'

'What were you looking for, then?'

'To see how far you had to come with it. I'd come half-roads to meet you,' said Willie.

The abuse he brought upon himself! And yet, when the great slabs of soda scone, butter and jam were filling his face, he paid less heed to the lecture than he did to the flies that swarmed about his oddly-shaped head.

At harvest and sometimes at haymaking, when the fields being worked were far from the steading, to save time in the tramp to and fro, meals were often brought to the place of work. More than one person had to carry the utensils. Great numbers of bowls and plates were brought in pan baskets, pots of broth or soup, potatoes, stew, custard, apple tart. These occasions were something of a picnic, but the men who ate their meals in the field thought little of picnics. They preferred the midday visit to the kitchen, the five-minute smoke in the cool shade of the stable. Here, in the open, when the meal was over, a man had to smoke in the broiling sun. He could go and take a drink at the well in the hollow, brushing the trailing grass from the spring and lying full-length to scoop up the water with his hands, but somehow a meal outside made the day endless. Even when they were able to have an extra five minutes, snoozing on their backs, they disliked such days. For my part, I always loved them. I loved them more when I returned to the steading late in the day and rediscovered its old magic, the way the buildings huddled together, the ranks of stacks in the stackyard, the calves bellowing for their evening meal and the tired dog dozing on the flags of the steps down to the pump. There was something wonderful, too, in standing at home and watching the others coming back at the end of a day, a day on the moss march, following a reaper cutting lying corn, a day in the Wee Five Acre, out of sight behind the row of tall ash trees, a day on the far hill with a clattering binder crossing and re-crossing a slope. I think it was partly the happy-to-be-home look on the faces of the workers that made a pleasure of this encounter. Those at home knew just the feeling of being out there on the far hill when the afternoon was running into evening; the feeling that soon they would be in the kitchen with as much porridge and cream as they liked to sup before the milking was over and supper proper was on hand. Often in the evening the men would go out to the Wee Field's fence and stare across at the far hill. It was beautiful wherever one stood, on the far hill above the low planting, looking at home, or at home staring at the evening mist forming in the hollow and hearing the owl's cry out there where dusk was gathering.

In the last days of winter or the first of spring the partridges pair. Winter and spring have a demarcation on a calendar but in the year they are a breath of warmth across a hill, the snowdrops wild on the fringe of a wood, a primrose opening and the partridges rising from the fawn of an old stubble hill and sailing down over a hedge to a new territory. Spring is in the hedge and the mellowing day just as the last of winter is in the solitary woodcock springing from the beech leaves and going off

in his heavy twisting flight through the spaces between trees and bushes.
In these early days of the year the first partridge pair would come to the
Wee Five Acre, along the hollow, fast, windborne, swinging up to clear
the drystone wall, gliding into its shelter and going on, as beautiful as
anything that flies, to the tall broom, the lean thorn on the Wee Five
Acre's edge.

There is a miracle to be seen in spring when a pair of birds begin to
frequent a nesting ground. They are there by chance, there in the breeze
before noon, when the day still has that chill in it and half a threat that
frost will congeal the mud by the gate before nightfall. One day goes
into another, the plough is carted home, the harrows sleep in the corner
where soon a crop of weed will hide their ugliness, the first shoots of oats
are carpeting the hill. The day they came by chance is forgotten. They
belong to the field, rising from it in the morning or just before dusk. Walk
down the hedge at nightfall and they will burst into the air and sail across
the march wall, gone, you might think, forever. At first light of day you
will find them in the same spot once more. Did they wander back in the
dark? When darkness was about the place did they delicately pick their
way under the poles of the gate and steal into the young grass, or did
they never leave at all? Watch these little chickens of the field in the Wee
Five Acre. They have all that is beautiful in their shape, their colouring,

their dainty movement. Think of the bantams of the farmyard, the fussy broody hen, and then look again at these neat brown fowl, so bright of eye, so alert. A poem should be written about them.

On the high side of the Wee Five Acre there is a sort of shoulder below the wall. On the shoulder grows an assortment of bushes and weeds. The foxglove stands a yard from the yellow dock, a gorse bush crouches close by a low blackberry. There is a crop of stones and a rabbit warren, a place where a weasel lives and, lower down this boundary, a dry ditch hidden by the wall on one side and a jungle of gorse and thorn. Along this dry ditch the hunting dog sometimes prowls. Sometimes a rabbit goes through it, but the partridges keep away. Out in the field, where they belong, they can see their enemy. They can run or throw themselves into the air. When the nest is made it may be on the high side of the field, close to the low blackberry or the gorse, but it will be in a place that is safe from the hunting weasel and the foraging carrion. The birds are in no hurry. It is spring, early summer. Already the plover has had her young. On the Switchback a hare has two offspring hidden somewhere in the ryegrass, and at the bottom of the Five Acre the yellowhammer has eggs in the ditchside nest. The showers of April obscure the far hills and the early blossom is in the orchard when the nest is made beneath the blackberry. Like the nest of the plover, it is no more than a hollow in the ground, a strand of grass or two, the fibres from the furrow, the leaves that survived the winter. The hen crouches there with her first egg, screened by the soft green leaf of the budded briar, the protecting arm of the blackberry. Look at her. She is there, a blend with all about, greyness and warm brown, a mark of rich chestnut, buff, fawn, feather lapping feather and all matching the colour of the ground, the shrivelled leaves that fell last autumn, the brown earth spread by the mole or the rabbit, the very dust of the field carried by yesterday's warm wind. Walk to the bush and stand there. The little heart of the hen will beat a thousand faster beats but she will stay there. Come again tomorrow and she will rise and burst into flight. Look at the flight and even that is beautiful, the tail spreads in the first second. Had you the quick sight of the hawk you

might see the rich tint of the tail feathers, the warm brown of the fox,
brighter than the back of the stoat, as red as the squirrel in the sunlight.
The wings bend to the ground and beat the air so fast that every hundred
yards or so the bird must glide, as though to take a breath. Watch her go,
away across the drystone wall, off with the contour of the field, smaller
and smaller. The field of young turnips takes her. The sorrel sways where
she alighted and you are alone by the blackberry bush looking down at
that warm hollow, at the fawn and olive-tinted egg, the first of a dozen.
Here on the Five Acre this covey is born. The weasel with all his cunning
never gets their scent. He hunts the mouse and robs the lark, he spoils
the home of the shrew and eats many a blind and helpless litter, but
the nest of the partridge escapes him. Even the plundering hedgehog
passes them, for when the bird is away she leaves the nest screened by
leaves and grass. The eggs are hidden in the brown debris of last season,
warmed by the summer sun and the breeze that sets the thorn scraping
the stones of the wall. When the brood hatches they are able to leave
the nest at once. When the stoat hunts, the clucks struggle into the grass
round about. They crouch there, brown and fawn and buff, motionless,
aware of danger by instinct. The hen does not desert them, but flutters
off a yard or two and stretches her neck so that she can keep her eye
on the nest. If man comes she may steal into the longer grass and hide,
or rise and fly into the air and flutter down again. Walk after this mad,
demented little bird and she will do it again and again until you are out
of reach of her brood. She is ready to die for them and often does.

We are not the only ones aware of the nest on the high side of the
Wee Five Acre. This nest has value. Willie had his eye on the eggs, but it
slipped his memory for a week and he was too late. The keeper has the
brood counted and Tom is thinking of September, thinking hopefully of
a covey of thirteen or fourteen birds sailing in and out of the Wee Five
Acre. Willie is too late. The keeper promises ten to his shooting party.
The mouth of the greedy world waters at the thought of these chicks,
but before summer is old one will die in the jaws of a cat, another will
be drowned in the bog, two more will fall to an out-of-season poacher

and the hawk may sweep in to slay another. They grow and learn to fly in this field, little models of their parents, every bit as neat and alert. In the morning they are picking their way across the dry turf, lifting a seed, taking an insect or a shoot of a sprouting seed. Past noon they are at the outcrop of boulder, dust-bathing, fluffing their feathers like the farmyard fowl. In the shadow of late afternoon, when the sun is up behind the hedge they are on that cool, sweet green turf in a little cluster. Can they see the far-off hills, the haycarts on the distant meadow? Does the linnet on the top of the hedge mean anything to them, the musical note of the goldfinch have beauty and sweetness that it has for man? Surely in such a brief life sweetness must be sweeter, the sun more radiant, the contrast between light and shade more acute?

The one that dies as the hawk strikes leaves his feathers tumbling in the breeze. The breeze dies and the grasshopper sings again and the pattern is complete. This morning the caterpillar of the moth died to feed the partridge chick and now the partridge is dead to feed the hawk. Soon the hawk will fall to the keeper's gun and its body will make a breeding ground for an insect that will feed a bird.

The reaping machine has gone from the meadow and the depleted covey sails out of the Wee Five Acre for the last time. Now they are at home in the shelter of the turnip field. They belong to the dancing leaves of the swedes, the tunnels between the furrows. Sometimes at evening the cock or hen will be on the pasture. The family will be called together by that scraping call that is summer as much as the flight of the swallow from the cartshed door. When the corn is down and the apples are ripe in the garden, the shooting party will come over the hill and walk the turnip rows. The covey will run ahead, hurrying for the ditch, the hole in the wall, the last hedge of sorrel and milk thistle, before they hurl themselves up to cross into the next field. The guns will roar and blast. A hail of six or seven shot will scream after them and some will fall, turning in the air and then thumping into the weeds. A cock bird and three hens may escape to skim on wildly to the potato patch. One of the hens may be too slow to rise from this shelter when the line comes down, but three may fly on, away over the stubble hill, off into the open places where they cannot be taken unawares, save at dusk when the man with the net is padding out across the pastures for them. The winds of winter will blow the down from the last dead thistle, the leaves of the thorn will fly to the farthest corner of the farthest field and these three birds will live and survive by swinging up over hedges, planing along the side of a dike, stealing away into the rushes on the fringe of the bog. In the last days of winter they may encounter another covey. The fight for hens will begin, a fight as full of bluff and bluster as the fights of the farmyard cockerels. When the sun melts the rime on the sleeping rowan and the first whisper of the new season is in the dormant hedge a new pair, the descendants of the first, will glide over the march wall to settle in the Wee Five Acre.

The Wee Field may have been in crop before I was born – I cannot remember ever seeing it under the plough – but the rest of the farm was cropped in rotation. Each field was cultivated for three successive years and then reverted to pasture. First it was ploughed as ley, that is, first year in corn, then it was put in roots and finally it was 'sown' out. When a field was ley it was hard to plough. It had been trodden hard by cattle. It was well manured. The sheep had grazed it, the milkers had fed over it a thousand times. It was ready to repay the rest. When it was broken the ploughing was the hardest task of the 'back end'. First the headland scrape was made and the rigs marked. This was done by making a sort of false furrow with an extension from the plough. The rigs were paced or measured with a rig pole and finally the ploughing proper was started. When a field has not been broken for several years the first ploughing with a horse team is hard on both horses and man. A man who has ploughed a field before knows the boulders and the stony places, but a man who is fresh to the acre goes warily. Today, of course, the tractor pulls the plough. It promenades to and fro turning three or four furrows at a time. When I was a youth ploughing took all the hours of late autumn and winter. I remember first putting my hand to the plough stilts in the bog field. It was to be a sown-out field. The corn to be sown would contain a mixture of grass and clover. When the oats were cut there would be an aftergrowth of fine grass to lay the foundation for pasture for next summer. How easy was this ploughing! The earth was soft, it turned to the coulter like a paring of soft cheese and steamed in the red sunlight of morning, so that when I look my breath at the end of my first furrows, the land smoked and I had that grand feeling of achievement a man feels when he is part of the scheme of farming. I had only to hold steady and allow the old horses to take me along the field. It was not hard to keep straight. Up and down we went and made great progress. The horses were such a fine team that they turned in together as one. I was proud of myself when the tea basket came and I could bask in admiration of my achievement. Unfortunately, no one was very impressed. After all, a fool like Willie could plough a sown-out field. I was from London. I was 'clever'. Surely a clever young man could hold a plough straight and make 'a hand' of turning a furrow? Towards the end of the day, when I had enough soil caked on my boots to make them feel like a deep sea diver's equipment, I began to think more of poor Willie. He did not tire so easily. His furrows at night were as straight as those he set up in the morning. My own had a decided tendency to become wavy! However, a day or two of this work satisfied me: I could plough and plough with horses as many a good man had done before me. But I had yet to break a virgin field!

Years passed. The bog field went to pasture. It grazed the milkers and the sheep. Carts jolted across it to the bog for rushes when stacks needed thatch. The surface became as hard as a road. Late in autumn one year I went back on a sort of a holiday. I had a day or two shooting, a day after wild duck on a cold, faraway loch. I mouched the home fields and poached into the territory of neighbours until the keeper became almost demented with rage. At last, feeling I must show I had the blood of my ancestors in my veins, I offered my soft hands to the plough. I think it was the scorn that made me determined. I might be soft. I might blister easily, but I had a good straight eye. They nodded. They could not deny the eye. The keeper swore my eye was too good when his pheasants

were in range, but to plough a field that had been fallow for years, that was man's work! Man's work – the old bog field that I had ploughed when no more than a boy. Why, I knew every rock and stone on it. I knew the run of every hare that crossed it and the nests of half the mice into the bargain! Nothing could stop me. They were persuaded. I was a ploughman. I had written a book about a ploughman. It was fitting that I should plough. The team was ready in the stable. The plough was already on the field. I went to the stable, brought out the pair of Clydesdales, slung the lines of one on to the hames of the other and scrambled up on to the mare's back. I went to the bog field in the brilliance of a November morning. The sun was a red fire in the east, the ash trees were bare and there was a light mist on the land. When I reached the field I slithered down and yoked the team to the plough. 'Hup, high, Mary, Prince, out of that!'

The coulter broke into the earth. I gripped the handles of the plough and set my jaw. Oh, the sad disillusionment. The team was pulling. All their energies were directed to putting the plough through stone-hard earth. They forgot to walk in a straight line. I could not keep the coulter breaking at an even depth. Up went the handles, drumming on my ribs, jarring my teeth. I yelled to the horses to stop, dragged the plough back, levelled it and started again. Almost at once it slipped out of the soil and we were slithering away at a half-trot! I panted and struggled, fought and groaned. My second furrow was no better than the first. When I had mastered the way of ploughing hoof-hammered land I was weary to death. The morning tea came when I thought night was due. The following day I went shooting again. I skulked the woodside, hung daydreaming on the march fence, did strenuous things like setting a dozen snares or watching a rabbit out on the moss. I kept away from the bog field, going no nearer than the Switchback Hill. It looked as it had looked years before, the black-brown earth steaming in the winter sunlight, the heads of the horses nodding as they plodded up the furrow, a gull or two flying behind.

The first-year crop of the bog field grew rich and strong. The straw was tall, the heads thick and hard. It ripened from pale yellow to almost white. When it was ready the roads were opened and the binder brought down. The day the binder was trundled into the field, it rained and blew a gale. The straw keeled over and the whole crop slowly became a mat. It was useless to think of using a binder. Parts of the field would have

to be scythed and the rest cut with a tilting reaper and hand tied. My brother and I were given the work on the reaper. I did the tilting with a rake and my brother drove the horses. We began one of the most heartbreaking tasks a farmer can face. It rained and shone alternately. When the rain stopped, the sun blazed down. In the dry spells, a day

or a day and a half, we all worked like lunatics. The reaper tore round
the field and the lifters had hardly cleared the last sheaf before the next
batch was thrust out. The horses were an old one and a young one.
Once the young one decided to run off. He turned into the standing corn
and bolted with his ears set back on his head. We careered through the
field like Roman charioteers. I dared not put the machine out of gear
for fear of smashing the only means of harvesting the half-ruined crop.
After a while the sheer agony of pulling a cutting reaper at full gallop
subdued the young horse and he stopped. Back we went to the perimeter
to resume the mad race against the weather. No summer was ever so
endless and yet so short. When the field was cut we had a day or two
preparing slack butts and then we hurried to fork the corn to the carts.
Is there any task as endless as forking acres of corn? When the last sheaf
went up we looked at the calendar. Tomorrow morning we were due
on the London train. School opened on Monday. What a grand tan we
had, but it was halfway through term before we recovered sufficiently to
remember that we had been promised a day or two's shooting at the end
of harvest. For us there had been no end to the harvest. Someone else
would get after the covey from the Wee Five Acre or stop the hare that
ran from the bog field to the Switchback Hill.

'Good boys,' I can hear grandfather saying, 'they worked heart and
soul at harvest.'

There was no other way. Harvest was a family affair. If we had half a
dozen Irishmen we always needed the family to help out. The activity in
the stackyard was as great as the activity in the field. Here in the bog field
two forked sheaves, two built carts and one led horses. In the stackyard
one forked to the stack, one built the stack and another raked round. In
the kitchen they made tea and carried it out. Bowls were laid down in
odd corners, fresh bowls were brought out and lost in the straw. When
it was all over, the stackyard was as neat as grandmother's bun when
she went to church on Sunday. The stacks stood in neatly thatched and
roped rows, round and cone-topped with just a little run out from base
to thatch. The only square-sided stack was a 'sow' stack of straw and

that as smart as any stack of hay or corn.

I used to look forward to the end of harvest. It meant that the days were my own. I had only two or three before my holidays ended, and what risks I took! I poached as far and as fast as my legs could carry me. Sometimes before report of my doings had reached the owners of the land concerned I was already back at school. I would get news of their reaction by letter from grandfather: Old X was heard saying that you had been poaching there. I sent word that you had been in London this while back and he must be mistaken. I doubt you'll have to watch what you're doing when you come again.

On my return the first thing I did was to lift the gun and hurry for the march wall!

From the end of the low planting to the far corner of the bog runs the burn. It brings water to almost every field. At its source it helps to drain the moss. Here the rain gathers in pools, pools that are half full of green moss. The bright spring sky is reflected in the pools. The little weathered shoulders of peat make nesting places for the birds of the moss and sometimes a mallard drake and a couple of ducks will alight to feed in the misty rain at dusk. The moss gathers water. Long ago its resources of peat were exhausted, leaving many a depression. The square face of the cutting crumbled and fell into the pit, making a bog. Above these bogs the wild cotton plant began to grow. On the fringe the round rushes grew in clumps. Little paths were made by hares and rabbits crossing the firmer ground. These paths, because of the nature of the ground, turned and twisted more than the loneliest country road. Between them the water was deep enough to take a man to the thighs. This acid, yellow-tinged water had to escape somehow. It drained slowly through the black earth to the corner of the low planting, and there the burn began, a filtered, bright little trickle of water materialising beneath a clump of fern, trickling along the stones of the ditch, gathering behind a boulder, making a home for the water bugs and the sinuous, yellow-green frog. At this corner the burn grows a crop that is lush and damp. The weeds are succulent, the myrtle grows profusely, cress fringes the stones and its white roots search the grit for life. The small birds know this drinking place. A rabbit regularly springs across from the wood to the hill and sometimes a pigeon comes gliding round to alight and drink among the drooping grasses. Twenty yards along the ditch the water gains speed. A drain from the hill gushes into its course. Oh, the cold water of a hill drain, how often has it quenched my thirst when the oatmeal and water were gone from the can in the shade of the dike.

Past the drain there is a sort of a ford. The banks of the ditch fall away. Cattle have walked here so often to drink that their feet have excavated the earth. Where they have stood in the ditch a sort of pool has formed, a deeper place, a waterhole. The burn murmurs as it leaves the pool and tumbles over the little dam of stones. On either side a forest of bracken rises. The water of the burn is kept for ever cool in this leafy shade. Willie, thinning turnips on the hill, likes to take a break and come down here to drink. He clambers into the ditch, takes off his cap and swats at the surface of the water to clear the creepers and the debris of green life. The water is as sweet as the air. He drinks and wipes his mouth, pauses, listens to the song of the bird in the tree and drinks again. It is young summer on the hill and life is good. The water of the burn goes singing on, a bird's feather speeds on the top of the current, twisting and turning, away through the tunnel of bracken and then out into the boggy banks by the potato patch, where the rich grass overhangs like

a schoolboy's fringe and is combed along in the burn's urgent course. Here the waterhen feeds out in the field. When man comes she hurries for the burn, running like an old lady catching a train. Once at the ditch the waterhen knows how to vanish. She is down in the water in an instant, along the bank and into the roots of the overhanging tree. She follows the water, through the crowding blackberry, under the beard of the whins, away in the secret places where the grass does not grow and the black peat bank is mined by the vole and here and there a rabbit hole comes out right above the water. The bird does not stay long but hastens on, under the bridge at the slap, through the walls of well-built stones and under the bulk of railway sleepers. The feather that floated like a tiny ship has been caught up by a quivering limb of round rush and is left far behind. When the man who saw the waterhen on the turf comes to the edge of the burn he stares for a while. The little backwater where the weed is thickest is discoloured with black mud. Here the bird splashed from the bank, but she is gone. The burn flows steadily on, gathering another drain and another from the red pipe that thrusts out of the bank every twenty yards or so. Beyond the bridge the banks are wider apart. The weeds and grasses can no longer obscure the bottom. The fine grit turns and tumbles in the current, a caddis grub in armour moves slowly on the bottom, a beetle crawls under a stone. More hillocks of gorse and a rocky cliff above the water, more tributaries from the drains and soon the burn can make a home for its first eel.

The eel lives under a slab of stone. Most of the day it lives in the recess beneath the stone, but when the sun is on the water, or some special flavour is in the stream, it moves out and goes weaving along to burrow into a little mound of mud. The mud streams in discolouration and the eel finds its food in the mud, taking the beetle or the larva of the fly, a hunter in the eerie world of muddied water. After a while it returns to its sheltering stone, backing into its home until only the tip of its head protrudes. When the heron comes stalking along the burn, the eel's head will be withdrawn. The heron will stand there waiting his time, patient as only a master angler can be patient. There is no morning, noon or night when this happens, only hunger and the chances of survival. If the heron is to survive he must take his eel or trout fry or vole somewhere along the burn's course. If the eel is to survive he must remain beneath his protecting slab of rock. The heron waits, the eel waits, just as the hunting cat sits endlessly above the home of the mouse.

Farther down the Wee Field the burn opens out. It is again a great watering hole. On one side its banks are broken and treacherous. On the other the bank is held up by the roots of a great old thorn hedge. Among the roots live a score of water voles. The waterhen has found a jutting rock and built her nest upon it, the wagtail has her home a few yards away and even the farmyard ducks climb this hedge bank to lay

their eggs in the tangle that grows at the bottom of the thorns. The speed of the burn is less. The wider area of water is no longer cold, but tepid in summer. Its edges are fringed with a sort of tideline of duck feathers. The broken banks on the Wee Field side are roosting places for the duck. They have a dozen flattened places that are the imprint of their bodies. Half the day they sit there, snoozing. At times they launch themselves into the burn and swim to and fro. They feed on the bottom, preen themselves and come paddling out at a shallow place, a procession to the farmyard just before feeding time. Beyond this place the burn rushes under the old road. Here its course is darkened, its banks steep and rocky and hanging with gorse and stunted bushes. In spring every few yards along the bank is to be found the nest of a bird. The yellowhammer nests in the grass, the linnet in the gorse, a chaffinch in the thorn.

I used to take a delight in following the burn's course in spring or early summer, discovering the nests. Year after year a score of birds were reared in the burnside. I would sit down on the grass between two clumps of gorse and peer along the burn, seeking the likely nesting spots with a practised eye. Often as I approached one of these places the bird would dart out from her nest and I hardly needed to look for its exact location. Often I was able to get to a point of vantage and look down into the nest. What masterly work is done with the hair from the horse's mane or tail and a few fibres of grass. Most numerous along the burn were the yellowhammers, whose scribbled eggs are wonderful to look upon. Schoolchildren believed that the eggs bore some message. I was never able to discover the exact message. Its subject was either love or death.

The burn, after making a couple of waterholes in the Sow's Field, runs under the march wall, waters the neighbouring field and comes back into the old road field before the quarry. Where the water leaves the old road field to go into the bog field, and later the bog itself, lived a large eel. Perhaps the water lower down ran too shallow and into too many streams for him to find his way back to the sea. He was a fine specimen. It was impossible to get at him, for he lived under the foundation of the march dike, too cunning to be taken by the patient heron, growing bigger as time went on.

Less than a hundred yards inside the bog field the burn began to grow tired of its banks. Its course and bed were hard and rocky. In time, with the drains of the hollow breaking to help it, it washed through at a weak spot and flowed into the round rushes. Here the snipe came, here the duck alighted and a marshy barrier protected the hillocks of harder ground where the hare could sleep. In the years I knew this spot I saw the work of the burn, saw the bog becoming deeper, more as it had been a thousand years before. Among the round rushes a reed or two shot up, a wild iris grew, a bed of the greenest weed began to spread itself and the place became dangerous at nightfall. Once I shot a duck there and almost plunged in to my neck trying to recover it.

The bog has its own life. Where the water spreads there are beds of black earth, earth that bears the tracks of the dainty water birds, the tracery of the feet of the jack snipe and his bigger brother. I crossed the bog one morning and shot a jack snipe for the first and last time. What delicate little creatures they are. Why they are shot I do not know, for there is scarcely a picking on their little bones. Their flight differs from that of the common snipe, for they are less wild. They arise, fly round and alight only a few yards from the place in which they were first flushed. When I had the jack snipe in my hand I was sorry I had brought him down. He weighed nothing. He was beautiful but he belonged to the bog and the marsh, a will-o'-the-wisp thing of the mist and the quiet morning.

Few people ever see the snipe on the ground, just as many more hear the corncrake without ever knowing what he is like. Perhaps the most secretive of all birds is the water rail. He is commoner than the countryman thinks, but he steers his way through the rushes and reeds and is gone, like a cunning old poacher or the fox in the thick bracken. The first time I ever saw the water rail was in the bog. It was a dead bird, stretched across a little patch of yellow round rush. I picked up the carcass and examined it. The water rail has something of the waterhen about its build. It is a finer thing and its whole appearance goes with its secretive habits. Its body seems unbalanced, for its thighs are short and its legs long in the lower joint. Its beak is red or orange in hue. The brown of its back is not unlike the brown of a hen pheasant and on its sides it has grey and white feathers that give the impression of horizontal, alternate bars of these colours. Its front is grey, the grey of a mouse. On the tail is a mark of white. It is an odd thing that both the little water rail and the waterhen have this touch of white, although the contrast is much greater in the waterhen than in the rail. On the ground the rail runs quickly. Its flight is low, a sort of scurrying away through the weeds or along the course of the water. It does not go far. Like the jack snipe its flight is short, but try to find a water rail once it has entered a marsh! The toad that jerks his way into a pool submerges and blends with the weed and mud about him, but the water rail vanishes. No dog can find it. Its elusiveness is God's gift to its kind. The chicks of the waterhen have it, the young of the plover. The master of camouflage and concealment does his work as only a master can. The helpless things of the world are well protected.

All the toads of the countryside seemed to gather in the bog at breeding time. They did not all belong there, for their colouring indicated that some had come from redder earth and places at some distance. Every few yards had a toad or two. There among the short rushes one would be sitting in meditation, its throat dilating, its liquid eyes unblinking. What a hunting ground for the heron, and yet the heron was not fond of the bog. He was much oftener on the burn, wading his way along, rising, when disturbed, with heavily beating wings and the harshest cry in nature. The curlew and snipe did not nest here. They were creatures of the higher ground, the moor and the moss under the open sky, where the watchful cock bird could command a view to the far horizon. The bog is a place of the more secretive waterfowl. A wild duck goes to and from her nest in a mysterious way. It is one of the best concealed. The nest is there among the tall grass, buried in feather and down and hay. The duck sits motionless throughout the brooding period, leaving the nest only at feeding times. When the young are born they rise with their mother and toddle away, a family of downy creatures, mottled with a wonderful yellow and brown. If the duck is forced into the air the family will disperse into the surrounding cover and somehow the mottle will prove to be the very colour of the place to which they go, a place where the leaves are brown, the roots of the rushes and reeds have yellow among them, fawn and mottled decay. There is no intense black in the field, no startling contrast of blue and scarlet. In places where colours are freakish no wildlife exists.

The bog was not all dangerous ground. It had patches that were firm and hard, arid hills where the gorse was stunted and the matted grass as dry as tinder. Here the ants lived, an adder basked. On the old bank of the burn – the course still carried a trickle of water – the slow-worm, not snake but lizard, lived beneath a stone. One of the greatest pastimes I had as a child was in lifting large boulders. The space beneath a stone is often the home of a mouse. Certainly a beetle will live there and once I lifted a large rock to remove the roof and part of the wall of the home of a pair of field voles. At first these furry creatures remained curled up. I wondered whether they had been asleep. They moved with great speed when they went. The house had a dozen exits. I stood long after they had gone, admiring the smooth wall of their tunnels, the wider cavity where they were in the habit of sleeping, a sort of chamber with room for two. Afterwards I replaced the rock and wondered if they would return.

My curiosity about these things was always great, but when I should have been on my way back to the bog to see if the voles had recovered from their fright, I was investigating the home of a wild bee or the more complex system of an anthill. The endless activity of an anthill could engage my attention for an afternoon. Who appoints the colony its tasks? When a stone is lifted the workers begin to remove the nearest 'egg'. The crumbs of earth that fall in their path are lifted and moved with amazing ease. In an hour the pupae have gone and the colony has removed to a lower level. Their tunnels are a work of art.

The milk cart has gone. Bright, fresh summer morning is rising behind the steading, silhouetting the hedge beyond the burn in the Sow's Field. In the court someone is carrying a can of mash to the piggery, but the activity is round a pair of carts, carts that are being railed and roped for bringing home a load. They are off to the bog for thatch, the thatch that was cut a fortnight ago and stands there in neat green sheaves, a harvest of a special kind. We wander to these carts and climb aboard before they leave. The carter welcomes us, because we can dismount and open and shut the gates on the way. He stands on the floor of the cart and urges the mare on. We sit on the fore-end and are jolted and vibrated until the chattering of our teeth becomes painful, but what smooth, comfortable contrast when the cart leaves the road and cuts across the old road field, leaving the train lines of its tracks on the soft turf.

This is a day on which it is grand to be alive. The man holding the reins may be considering that it is Saturday or that today the grocer will be at the road-end with his ounce of twist or his plug of chewing tobacco, but our thoughts are on the brilliance of the morning, on the greenness of the rushes, the song of the bird. Down there in the bog a finch is searching for seeds on a bed of early-maturing weed, a hare is loping in the sunlight, going leisurely away in the safety of the ear-high forest about him, crossing the little clearings, leaving his print on the soft black earth.

The carts come to a halt as soon as their wheels begin to sink. The horses search the rush stubble for something to eat, the fine, tender grasses that grow between the clumps, as sweet as the dew, a pastel shade of green that belongs to the marsh. We are not eager to carry forkloads of rush sheaves to the cart. The first waterhole takes us over

the boot heads, and once our feet are wet we might as well explore. The bird that rose so fast was a nightjar. He was sleeping by the stone heap on the little hill. He is going away fast, across the bog, over the alders yonder, on to some new sleeping place, for the sun of the morning is not his world. He is a creature of the half-light, purring on the moss when the sun has gone and the crepuscular world is awaking. The nightjar goes. A yard ahead of the gorse bush a hare comes into full view. He cocks his ears, turns and takes the trail back. Perhaps as he runs he is waiting for the sound of a shot whining above his ears, but we have no gun. We have come to look at the roosting place of a family of partridges driven from their home by a mowing machine, to study the tracks that abound on the little hillocks, to put up a duck snoozing the day away and send a pair of snipe swerving and 'scarping' into the morning sky.

Look back now across the bog, to the brow of the bog field where the cart tracks show. There are eight lines where there were four. The rush loads have gone. The little stooks have been lifted and the bog's harvest is in. Here we are, far beyond the range of the noon whistle, in this great depression that grows water weed, rushes, blackthorn and alder. At the boundary a few tall gorse bushes grow. The breeze moves them and when we catch a glimpse of that movement with the corner of our eye we gasp at the thought of someone watching us from behind the drystone wall, someone about to climb over and come to us. We are in a lonely place. The two farms we can see are more remote than the home steading. Down here no beast lows, no dog barks, and after a while we are glad to turn again and make our way to the firmness of the pasture, to see a tall and somehow friendly ash, and, at last, the whitewashed gables of home with the kitchen chimney giving that trickle of smoke that denotes that the midday meal is already cooked and our places at table laid and waiting.

The drystone walls were built long ago by a man who had time for such a task. He was a man with a good eye, a capable man who could turn a boulder in his hands and see at a glance the way it should be laid. I remember watching my grandfather building up a breach in the dike. He was not short of skill. As he lifted the stones he turned them completely so that he could see all their faces. As he put them down they were fitted into the wall so that they added to its strength and balanced securely. He was only doing a few feet of walling, but across the whole countryside ran thousands of miles of the dike-builder's art, along hollows, across ridges and up sheer brows, broad-based walls, lichen-grown, strong barriers to resist the charge of a bullock, steady, so that a man could climb over without risking his neck. The stones came from the fields.

Among the old country folk there was something of a belief that stones were a crop in themselves. In a way it is true. They grow in the soil. Ages ago the glaciers moved and churned the boulders to smoothness and roundness. They were spread across the earth where the glaciers moved. The ice age went. The scrub and forest began to crawl across the land, out of the valleys, up the mountains and the boulders were buried in vegetation, in the layers of earth that coated the land. Generations of ploughs have cut the pasture. At each ploughing a few hundred more stones are rooted from the subsoil to the top. The crop is as regular as the corn and the roots. It will continue so long as man ploughs, for he can never remove them all. Every field of every farm in such a district has its stone heap. In the dead days that are sometimes used for rolling grass ropes, cutting thistles or clearing ditches, a man is sent out with a cart to lift a few stones. It could be a sort of a punishment, a job for a man who has a habit of breaking his spade, putting his foot in a milk pail or cutting his hand with a sickle. Willie sometimes got sent to lift stones. He would fill a cart once or twice in an afternoon. No one supervised his work, for who could tell how many he had lifted when the stone heap looked like any other heap of stones, and the field always seemed to have as many on its surface as it had before any were lifted? Generations had lifted the crop of stone and enlarged the stone heap. Nature took care of the heap itself, for in time a briar seeded in the soil that blew into the stones and gorse sprouted beside dog rose and blackberry. No worthwhile soil was being covered, for a stone heap invariably sits on a scar of rock, an outcrop of the hill. No rabbit can live in a stone heap, but the heap has its own life. A weasel tribe asks for no better shelter, an adder loves a dry stony place. Somehow it is right that a snake that can kill a barefoot child, or a slinking beast of prey, should live in a dreary corner.

The stone heaps of all the fields had their weasels, their stoats, their odd snake, a few hundred beetles and other insects that lived round the roots of the dock and the pink-fingered foxglove. The weasels and stoats were hardly ever disturbed except when a gateway was being walled up, or a dike made higher to keep out a venturesome flock of sheep. When these jobs were done a cart would be wheeled to the heap and the stone lifted, loaded and taken away. The weasels were hard to find, for as the stones were shifted they scuttled on through the tunnels and funnels of their home. Somewhere in the heap they had their breeding place, their sleeping quarters, their bone-strewn larder. If ever I helped at such a job I did so nervously. I know that the bite of an adder is not often fatal and that a weasel can only nip a man's hand, but I was never able to overcome a childish fear of these two creatures. The sight of a snake still makes me shiver and the musky odour of a stoat or a weasel, or even a ferret, still makes me feel pity for the rabbit.

A weasel family will find dry quarters among the stones, whether they be the stones of a wall or the gleanings of the field piled in some infertile corner. It is hard to believe that anywhere above or below ground can be dry when the burn is in spate and the waterholes are growing bigger every day in the hollows, but the weasels and stoats are fond of dry places. They will creep away into the heart of a stone heap and seek out a sheltered, drained place where they can be comparatively dry.

Here they have young. Nothing living close to the home is safe for long. The mice disappear, the lark's nest is plundered, the young rabbits are slaughtered in their furry bed. They are alert day and night when the young are hungry.

Summer grows old, the young are fed and trained to hunt for themselves. For a while you may see seven or eight about the heap, and then the numbers diminish. A field can only support so many animals and birds in a wild state. The young weasels move away, taking over some deserted jungle of stones and straggling briar. The parents remain in their 'warren', venturing far along the hedge, far across the field in search of prey. You will see them only infrequently in summer, for when food is plentiful and grass and weeds are high, the hunt is brief and under cover. In winter, when the ground is hard, the pair will be out longer searching for the mouse, tracking the rabbit, slinking in and out of the dike to take the bird unawares. Is there anything more like the cold creed of survival of the fittest than the sight of a weasel looking at man from the shelter of a stone heap? The hard little eyes are like clear glass beads. The neck is arched, the fangs show on either side of the whiskered mouth, the lips are the thin lips of a relentless creature and its life is lean and hard, like its body. Put him in a coop with a dozen fluffy chicks and in no time his mask will be red with the blood of all of them.

I have often listened to the stories of the havoc of a fox in a chicken run, but I doubt whether the fox has the tigerish killer in him that stares out of the face of a weasel or a stoat. They know no law but necessity. When they kill the ground bird's young in summer they are behaving as winter taught them to behave. Winter was long on the field. The cold fingers of the gale stabbed and fumbled through the stone heap. The mouse hibernated in some place hard to find, impossible to scent, and the linnets and sparrows flew in wary flocks, rising from the pasture like leaves in the wind. Winter was long and a lean stoat or weasel gets murder in his blood. When the fullness of summer comes he takes his toll of the careless life about him, and many a bird comes back to find that the grasshopper sings a senseless song and blood and feathers are all that remain in the nest.

There are many accounts of weasels hunting in packs. I have seen a family hunting a dike together in much the same way as a ferret will work its way through a burrow. One or another of the family constantly appeared on the side on which I was standing. The hunting went on even although more than one of the family saw that I was there. The first to see me paused, reared up and looked at me, as though considering me as a prey. After this inspection it ignored me, entered a hole in the stones, explored it, came out and went through the dike to the other side. Another did the same thing. The hunt moved on. I could only imagine they were having a sort of drive along the wall. I could see no sign of mice or of any animal that might have been the quarry, but I wondered if an entire family of mice, or even a pair of voles might be moving on ahead, scurrying along the secret paths in the heart of the wall, aware that the chase was on and the killers drawing nearer at every fresh minute. When this hunting family were well ahead I moved after them, hoping to see their quarry. Although they explored every inch of the wall I saw nothing ahead of them and I concluded that they were hunting in the same way as I often hunted myself, searching in likely places, walking the round rushes for a rabbit, the roots for a partridge, the woodside for a pigeon. I have always been an idler when in the fields and when a thing engrosses me I forget that I have a meal waiting at home or an appointment to have my hair cut. I went on up the dike. Somewhere I lost them. They ceased to appear on my side of the wall. I stood on the bank and looked over. They were not leaving on the other side. Somewhere, either in the wall or beneath it, they had come upon prey. I listened, prodded the stones, waited. The ground had swallowed them. The hunt was over.

Often a bird, chased by a hawk, will fly into a wall and take shelter. Often mice and the little creatures of the field will run to the wall. It is no wonder that a weasel likes to make his home in such a place. Even a rabbit, cut off from his burrow by dogs, will shelter in a wall or run right through it if there is a gap in the stones. In addition to these

creatures, the wall is the home of countless insects which are the food of weasels and the snake. Like the weasel, the snake can find a dry place under some foundation slab of rock. When the sun shines and the breeze is rocking the bracken at the side of the dike, the snake is out, sleeping in the warmth, coiled on the dry grass. On the colder, wet days, he retires to his shelter in the wall, as he does for the whole of winter and the greater part of the year. I have often wondered whether the bite of an adder is more dangerous after his hibernation or when he is strengthened and improved by the sun.

The pheasants came into all the fields and nested this year in one and next year in another. Several nests could be found on the farm in April and May. At nesting time the pheasants are hard to count. The cock is often in flight and the hens are stealing about the cover of the hedge and the gorse hills. The bird that nested in the March Gate Field came there when I was a small boy. I forget why I was there at the particular time. Perhaps there had been some bereavement in the family or some epidemic at school. At all events, I came when the plovers were nesting and stayed on until summer gave the far hills a tinge of purple that was the mass of heather in bloom. The spring rains sparkled in the pools in the hollows, the grass covered by the water was green as only grass in a wet country can be green. I paddled the pools. Sometimes they were warm with the sun on them all day. To have grass beneath my naked feet was one of the pleasures of my life. In a summer, with my boots or shoes slung round my neck, my feet would become so hardened that I could run over the hard stubble when harvest came. It was this kind of summer when I observed a pheasant as I have watched many birds since, a pheasant frequenting a place, making a nest – one which I did not discover too easily, hatching a family, feeding them across the little knowes where the ant nests were plentiful, and in the end taking them away for that terrifying adventure before the guns of the shooting party, to die or be spared as the partridge covey had fared a month before.

For almost a week I had been trying to locate the nest of a plover. The bird had risen in a number of places within a large circumference. Each day, without much method, I had sought vainly for this nest until I finally came upon it close to a little gorse bush. It contained four eggs. For some reason I decided the eggs were addled. I was looking at them when I saw the pheasant hen. She dropped into the field across the top of the hedge, walked a few dainty paces and went into the round rushes. A pheasant nest was something worth seeking. I hurried to the rushes and began my search. The hen came out on the far side of the patch and ran away along the field. It is exciting to see a pheasant running. They go arrowing over the ground, not as fast as a rabbit, but much too fast for a barefoot boy, no matter how fleet of foot. I watched her go and then resumed my wandering through the rushes. I was not without experience of the habits and behaviour of birds. I knew that because a duck rose from the bog it did not follow that she nested there, or that plover would lay in the dusty hollow I found on the ploughing. After a while I gave up and concluded that the hen had been passing over.

The following day I was in the field again, walking carefully towards the plover's nest in the hope of seeing the bird sitting on her eggs when I again saw the hen pheasant. She was running into the rushes this time. Patience is a thing a boy learns in the country. If a bird flies into a bush, sooner or later it will fly out. I watched for the pheasant. My eye took in every clump, every little rise, every hollow. Away on the far side of the rushes I glimpsed her. She was stealing up through two clumps of gorse, a fawn-brown ghost, without sound, with movement smooth and unobtrusive, like the swaying of the grass, gently, naturally.

A hunter must not run when he is stalking his quarry. He must move slowly and steadily like the quarry itself. Violent movement alerts the whole world. Go steadily, confidently and without haste, and you need never go hungry. Already I knew these lessons. I went down the slope, through the rushes, over the little knowes and up among the whins as a cat would have gone, and when I came to a little brow and a stone heap I looked over a sort of forest of gorse, gorse that was sun-drenched and spattered with yellow blossom. You have breathed the scent of gorse on a bright warm summer's afternoon. You know its drowsy fragrance, for it was made for soothing a man lying on his back, staring at the blue heavens and parading his dreams. Somewhere in this nodding green and butter-hue was the bird I had seen crossing the rushes. I began to walk gently round the gorse. There are a thousand likely places in a clump of gorse as big as a cottager's garden, places where the overhanging bushes cover bare earth, places where the thin grass is tall and dry, leafy places. Somehow all of them look like a hen pheasant sitting on her nest. Perhaps I looked at her more than once. Man is a blind animal. He can walk over the rarest plant and not see it. He can pass the crouching rabbit and only knows it was there when it goes bouncing across the field. I saw the hen when she was running away again. I spent the rest of the afternoon searching for her nest. Many a gorse thorn had to be pulled from the sole of one foot or the other, but at length I had to give up. I stood a little while recollecting where I had last seen the bird, the line I knew she had taken as she came to the gorse, the line on which she left. I think I was born with this sort of hunting mind. Perhaps we all have it; I do not know. When I went home it was with the thought of afternoon tea. I liked oven scones and butter almost as much as I liked being in the fields, and the fields I loved, and love with a passion that is with me yet.

I do not know how many days I spent in the March Gate Field. Every day, before noon or after noon, I saw the pheasant. I never saw her mate, but the story was there, just as the story was there when the plover rose in the same circumference every day. Gradually the moment when

I saw the bird narrowed the distance from the nest until I knew where it was within a yard or two. I went home and gave my news.

'A pheasant is nesting in the March Gate Field,' I told the family.

'Just so,' said grandfather. 'Up about the whins and the stones yonder. About three or four yards from the standing stone, near the roll of fence wire dial, lies among the whins.'

This sort of thing always took my breath away. Grandfather had more to do than seek the pheasant's nest. It was a thing my father might have done, for he was given to wandering the fields when he was at home.

'Grandfather had his eye on you out there,' said one of my aunts. 'He's been watching this day or two. He saw what you were after.'

The nest was where he said it was. I had not found it when I broke my news, but he had done what I had done, only at much greater range. He had seen the bird rise' more than once and had used his knowledge of the field. In the morning I found the nest. It already held live eggs. I did not go too close, hardly touched the sheltering gorse and peered down at it without disturbing the grass or making the smallest fragment fall into the hollow where the khaki eggs were lying. A pheasant hardly needs an excuse for deserting her nest. Startle her into flight twice or three times and she will abandon everything. I knew this. I would crawl as slowly and silently as a snail on a mossy stone to look down at that nest every day. The hen sat on her eggs without being aware that I watched her. Sometimes when she was away I was able to count them. She finished laying, began to brood. At home I was warned to leave her in peace while she brooded, but I was there the day before the first chick hatched. After that it was not so easy to get close to the family. The hen led them away. Two eggs remained unhatched among the shells of nine others. Something took the lives of two of the brood. Perhaps a hawk or a stoat or a living insect destroyed them. Perhaps they drowned, for a heavy rain made a death trap of the patch of round rushes that provided such handy shelter when they ran after their mother from the short grass. They grew in size, the suggestion of tails came soon after they became properly feathered. They looked like ragged partridges, then like small hen pheasants. They were all brown like their mother, for they were immature, and would be, even when October caught them on the turnip slope. When they were feeding like farmyard birds and as big as some of the season's hatching in the chicken run, they disappeared from the March Gate Field. They were off in the friendly cover of the corn, taking insects, wireworm and leatherjackets, a seed or two.

I saw them again for brief moments. When the afternoon sun was beating down and the hawthorn at the side of the cornfield was exuding that 'green' smell, the hen and two of her youngsters fluttered up and perched on the drystone wall before crossing into the moss. Another time I saw one flap up out of the corn and alight again, and wondered what was going on out there. Were they disputing among themselves, or had one encountered a weasel? The bird that rose planed forward a little way and settled. The corn was ripening. The ground beneath was dry, the stalks growing hard and bleaching. Summer was going and the petals falling from the blackberries.

When October came I was not there. The fields could teach me things no teacher could impart, but I had to have some arithmetic and the way of a lexicon. The postman brought us a parcel. Someone had been down the potato field or through the wood. A brace of pheasants. I stroked their wonderful plumage, admired the copper and black, the red of the eye, the white on the neck. I cried a little. I was young and soft of heart.

The moor, or the far moss, as it always was to me, was just another field, a field with a boundary that was the sky, a dead tree, a cairn on a little hill, a mound where the blaeberries grew. Out there I imagined all the wonders I could not find on my own doorstep. There the curlew nested on every bank, there the grouse nested, and somewhere in the grey rocks that stood in the dim distance the wild cat lived. The nearest I got to the mystery of this wild place was the peat diggings. Later, when my imagination was less keen, I crossed the far moss, shooting grouse. The wild cat was not there. The curlew had long since hatched. I discovered it to be a place where many a peaty pool reflected the slowly passing clouds, a place of silence, save for the bee in the heather and the crackle of heat in the woody roots and fibres.

When I went to the far moss to shoot I went by invitation. A friend of my grandfather's owned a farm out there, a sheep farm. The steading of this place crouched in an island of green grass, a few rough round hills that had been won from the moor, drained and cropped once on a time. When I knew them these hills were going back to their natural state. The heather was growing tall in the ditches and creeping up the hills. The farm, tenanted by a shepherd and his wife, was going back to the wild too. Great yellow docks grew in its court, nettles filled the cartshed. The doors of byre and stable had rotted and fallen away, for the steading was

only used when sheep were gathered and counted. In the dilapidated buildings I discovered rusty implements, bits of ancient harness and a broken gun. There were tins of tar used to treat such things as foot rot and maggot, and paint used for branding the blackface sheep. I stood with a gun over my arm looking at this old place and wondering about the people whose peat fires had blackened its chimney. The scrawny fowls picked their way about the turf, rabbits ran within yards of the door. Waiting for my companion to reappear from the farmhouse where he had gone to give news of our arrival, I put up my gun at one of these rabbits. I was sure I had it and walked to the fringe of bracken where it had tumbled. The ground was riddled with holes. The shot had put every rabbit out of sight, including the one I had shot. No doubt it had simply kicked itself into a hole. There were so many holes I could not tell where it might be.

My friend returned and we set off. The whole of the moss was pitted with burrows. Here and there a short tunnel ran through a mound. A rabbit would disappear and reappear again in a second. They were well used to the safety of their homes, for they did not stay below long if we fired a shot at them. A big hare rose from beside a clump of heather. He knew every bit of cover and sped off across a peat hollow, turned along another bank, slowed down and took it at his leisure. I had fleeting glimpses of him as he worked his way across the moss, going slower and slower as he put more distance between us. The grouse were hard to find. We walked a long way in search of them. Have you walked a moor after grouse? Oh, the way to shoot them is to have them driven, to sit comfortably in a butt and wait for them to come skimming down over the shoulder of the moss, to give them two barrels coming and two going. For this you need loaders and beaters, ponies to carry the luncheon baskets, newspaper men to record the bag! We were walking the moor, hoping for a brace of grouse or black game and the strength to go on until we had them. Walking the moor you climb out of a drain, cross a plain that is covered with a forest of heather, jump down into a peat digging, stumble on through water, over crumbled peat and fragments of ancient trees. It takes the breath, it makes the hands shake, the aim unsteady. At the very moment you are stepping up on to the next bank, a pack of grouse goes into the air. They rise with such a whirr of wings, such a shattering explosion of flight, that the nerve of the man with the gun is affected. He shoots late or too soon. The hard quills of the old lyre-tailed cock turn the lead. The pack sails out of sight. The next quarter of a mile looks just like the quarter of a mile behind, and far away the curlew makes his towering cry. Far away are the white-walled farms and the friendly green hills of the arable country.

Sometimes I have this feeling, even now. Once I went about with a gun. Now, less of a hunter than I was, I go with a fly rod. The fishing, for me, is always better in the faraway, inaccessible spot; in the lake in the heart of the mountains, where the trout are as old as the crags. I set out for these places full of hope. I have that warm feeling, knowing that I have the Greenwell, the Black Spider, the Peter Ross, in my box. I go to bring home the dark-hued fish that has grown fat in peace and has never seen the marvels of tinsel and cock's hackle. At some time in the day I look back at the landmarks of the places from which I have come and I know that, although I enjoy my solitude, I belong in the tribe.

The birds of the moor have little occasion to fly from their natural enemies. They sail down to a fresh bank of young heather every so often. They fly up when they are squabbling among themselves. The old cock bird crows and flaps to the top of the stunted thorn in the morning sun, but they keep to the ground most of the time, for they are birds of the ground. In August they fly more often, for in August the calendar marks the twelfth and the days of the big packs are numbered. The birds that rose before us had not been broken up by a shooting party, but the guns had sounded elsewhere and the memory of the old cock was stimulated. He led them away.

My companion halted and took his breath, looked at the way we had come and the afternoon sun on the far-off mountains.

'Is it worth it?' he asked.

I never ask myself this question. I have never been able to weigh my pleasure against a negative, the state of not doing what I am doing. I simply nodded. We went on, up the slope, over the hill. A moor is like a sea. It ends when a man is past being tired of the sight of it. This moor went on and on. Somewhere, away beyond the farthest rise, was a loch and a grey road. Before we reached the rise the black game were up once more. I was past excitement. I had time to pick the bird I wanted. I shot the cock and he came down with a thump on the heather.

Take the body of this bird of the moor in your hand. He is a little bigger than the cock pheasant. He has something of the plumage of the jackdaw on him, something of the blue sheen, he has the red eye mark and the domed head of the cock grouse. His tail belongs to an artist's sketch book. No other bird has such a tail. The tail of the pheasant is beautiful, the short stubby tail of the green woodpecker is wonderful, but the old dark moor cock was given this tail as a compensation for living in a wild place, under a sky that is often obscured in mist, often black and sombre. He makes his call from the safety of that great sea of heather and waterholes where the mist is winding and the blackface sheep are sheltering until morning.

I liked this trip to the far moss because, when I went, I could just see the hills of home. It looked as wonderful from this point as the moss did when I stood gazing at it from our own fields. Out in this wild place I could see the smoke of farms closer to the moss than our own, beyond them I could see the faint outline of the dikes and fields of home. The beast on the Big Hill was probably Mary or Prince, the two Clydesdale plough horses. I could see the tip of a tall elm, the fringe of the high planting. My mind could fill in the details, the burn in the hollow, the march gate, the chickens crowding round the mash can when the pigs were being fed, the pony taking great draughts of that clear, cold water in the pump trough. Distance lends enchantment – this thing has been said so often that it is worn out. It depends where a man stands. I used to love to stand far away from the fields I loved and to view them in perspective, seeing them from a new angle, the angle on the parlour gable, the kitchen gable or the sitting room gable, for the house was built in a T shape.

When I returned after such an excursion I felt the comfort of home, and home was anywhere between the march gate and the back of the Switchback. I could stand at the gate and look up the March Gate Field, knowing that in the tall gorse that nodded on the moss dike a twite had a nest, that the eggs were warm beneath the mother bird and the whole thing was snug there, swaying with the breeze. To come back always had this delight for me. Time could not alter it, for it was there if I returned in the bleakness of winter or the darkness of night. At night I could see the gloomy outline of the low planting and the light in the kitchen window. My aunts had an old-fashioned habit of leaving a light in the window for any member of the family who was out late. The wick burned low for me often as I struggled home, fumbling with the chains of the three gates and squelching through the potholes of the road.

The forest of the oatfield probably protects more helpless creatures in summer than all the other fields of the countryside. The time between sowing and harvest brings so many things to life in a state of comparative helplessness that, were it not for the cover of the growing crop, the preying animals and birds would slaughter them by the thousand. The owl hunts the open pasture, but scores of mice evade him, down in the security of the stalks of the oats. He could plunge down after them, but

the heads of corn would fold under his wings and protect the scampering mouse. He wastes no time over the corn. The kestrel, too, knows that it is useless to hover there and the stoat and the weasel do not venture to hunt because there the scents are confusing, the sounds are muffled by the gentle rubbing of a million stalks and the whispering of ten million ears of corn. The mouse thrives, the beetle goes unmolested, the larva develops, the fly hatches and harvest bug and harvest mouse live to believe that summer is for ever, an eternal breeze swaying the yellowing corn, the voice of the corncrake unending.

Life in the cornfield reaches that halcyon wonder of high summer that is in the serenity of the day before harvest. The bird sings in the thorn, the grasshoppers are in grand chorus, the seeds of the Scotch thistle that grew among the oats drift away as light as the small white clouds going off yonder above the highest of the mountains. How often have I seen it like this, the richness and ripeness of corn ready for the binder, covering the round outline of the Other Clutag Hill like the flaxen hair on the head of a small boy. The scythe sounds in the morning, when the dew is still in the thick bottom of grass, weed and clover, the sharpening stone rasps on the blade, the thin corn at the headland falls and the red and white of the sorrel flower topples with it. Somehow the sun seems brighter. A butterfly alights on a stone and flicks its wings, and the grasshoppers were never louder. When the roads are cut at evening the young rabbits are to be seen on that bare patch between headland and crop. The tracks they have used for months are laid wide to the sky. The great area in which the mouse ran is reduced and now the owl sits on the dike. He knows the signs. The story is an old one to him. The first foolish mouse to bustle from the wall to the corn will die. The young rabbits sit nervously in the fringe of the stalks, ready to run across the field rather than venture those four or five feet of stubble left by the man with the scythe.

In the morning, as the cutting begins, the ground vibrates with the giant tread of three great Clydesdales. The song of the grasshopper population is drowned by the clatter and rattle of wheels and running binder sheets. The mechanical arms cast out sheaves when the knotter and the knife have done their work, the work of hands. The butts of the sheaves are filled with the succulent green life that fed the rabbits, sheltered the mouse. Everything on the fringe creeps deeper into the field. The five feet at the headland becomes five yards, fifty yards. The partridges creep out at midday when the horses are led home for a trough of corn and a drink at the waterhole. They hurry off through the stubble, past lying sheaves and sheaves in stooks, to finally throw themselves up into the air and sail over the dike. A rabbit, isolated out there by that ring of tramping hooves and a noise like the end of the world, bolts for the ditch and the warren, but the mouse knows no other world but the vastness of the clover and grass beneath the tall trees of the oats. The pheasant hen has done what she will do in the open field

or in the wood, she has crouched in a hollow, trusting to her camouflage
to protect her. When the knives are close she will run out and launch
herself in flight, accompanied by her nearest neighbour. The small boy
playing in the stooks will catch a vole and search vainly for the shrew
after he has heard its shrill and frantic warning. In three or four days
the hill will be bare, the grasses drying in the butts of the sheaves, the
grasshoppers and beetles providing a grand banquet for the birds that
come between cutting and carting.

The very nature of harvest gives the life of the field time to recover.
The corn ripens and dries in the sheaf. Another field has to be cut while
cutting weather holds. The great change in the cut-down forest becomes
accepted. The mouse runs warily and the rabbit pops across the ditch,
for there is still a tasty bite in the undergrowth. The owls hunt when the
sun has gone from the western sky and the field sits sleeping. The habits
of the field have changed. Once the mouse and the shrew were safe and
ran about their world when the sun was up, but now they are back to
life as it is when the corn is shorn, and their habits are nocturnal. Even
the pheasant is on the stubble at sunset and sunrise, together with the
rabbits and the journeying hare, for who can say to what field or hill –
for that matter to what man – a hare belongs?

This thing would happen annually on the hills that were under corn,
the Low Planting Hill, the Other Clutag Hill, the Big Hill and the
Switchback Hill. The low fields, too, saw this change, but on two of the
hills, those adjoining the moss, when the corn was cut, the grouse came.
Harvest was always after the shooting began on the far moss, often in
late August. The grouse and black game were fond of a feed from the
stooks and announced their arrival night and morning with the cry that
was normally only heard up in the peat moss, away on the road to the
farthest hills and the rocks above the sea.

'Did you hear that?' someone would remark when the milk cart was
being loaded with cans. 'Grouse on the cornfield.'

I think the workman about the farm looked and listened for the
presence of game with the express intention of letting me know. Perhaps

they liked to see my reaction. They were never disappointed. If a hare rose more than once on the back of the farthest hill, or a pheasant burst out of the turnips, they had only to tell me to send me to that spot with a gun. I was not always successful. In a turnip field a pheasant has all the cover he wants and a hare has every tremor of the ground to warn him of man's approach. When they said they heard grouse on the corn hill I knew I had to be more wary than ever. The grouse feed on the ground as well as on the stooks. There is always a bird on the lookout. He sits with his head up, watching the world from the top of a sheaf or a high place on the dike. Sometimes, for the sheer joy of being alive on such a day, he will crow or cackle.

When they saw me coming the grouse would rise and go fast across the field, away to the far side of the moss. I would stand at the march wall staring after them, working out exactly where they had alighted and considering my chances of putting them up at that place when they were in gunshot. It meant a poaching expedition. I never thought twice about such a venture. A look to left and right, pause in the shelter of the Low Planting to listen to the drum of the wood, and I would clamber the wall or straddle the fence at the moss ditch. Often I was watched. Intelligence was passed to the keeper, but could he mark me down as he marked the covey? Tomorrow I might be off in another direction after a hare, or a pheasant. I would make for the dike that ran round the moss, creeping within range of the grouse as well as I knew how. Oh, the wariness of the grouse! I could be out of sight, in the safe cover of a wind carrying away the sound of my approach and they would rise before I was ready. Sometimes they must have glimpsed a movement behind the wall at a place where I fondly imagined I was under cover. Perhaps they became aware of a change in the background to a tiny hole, a space between the stones of the dike. Often I fired a shot after them and watched them go away with the wind. More than once they crossed the moss and settled close to the corn hill again.

It was possible to stalk them from the gate to the corn hill. At the gate a thorn hedge gave me cover. I would wriggle through and crawl

to the first stooks. My enthusiasm took me across the hill on my knees. Sometimes I crawled over a dead thistle and had my hands filled with thorns. I thought very little of the pain. I was used to this sort of discomfort. To get within range of a hare in the morning I often got drenched with water from the grass, frozen by the rime that covered the pasture. Stalking in the cover of the stooks I might take half an hour to make my way to the back of the field. A rabbit might rise and run ahead to warn the grouse, or my foot knock a sheaf from a stook, but now and again I was successful. I did not shoot from the ground. I liked to stand up suddenly, put my gun to my shoulder and take them as they went off. Sometimes the tail bird fell, sometimes the first one to present himself against the sky as he lifted himself to cross the dike.

Grandfather, when his eyesight was keener, could not resist the call of the grouse on the stubble. Once he employed a device that he had seen used when a boy. He harnessed an old horse in a cart, lay down in the bottom of the cart with his gun and steered by instinct to the field. An old horse knows what is expected of him. Put his head in the general direction he is expected to take and he will do the rest. Old Bob, the cleverest horse that ever lived, took the old man up the hill in the cart. The grouse fed happily. The look-out cackled and stood stupidly on the wall. When he was within range grandfather got on his knees on the bottom of the cart. He came back with a brace of grouse and the red glow of achievement on his cheeks. He was never tired of telling the story.

At the end of the ploughing, in the days before the tractor and easy transport to and from a field, the plough might be run up into a corner and left there. The sowing would take place, the harrowing and rolling. The crop would begin to grow, and in the stony corner the weeds would rise. It takes a fine, tall crop of weeds to cover a plough. The handles stick up towards heaven, more often than not, but in time the yellow weed grows to its full height and screens even these. The vetch rises, the undergrowth of soft cool weed creeps on, and in a little while the plough is buried. The growing weeds hold the rain and the dew when the rain clouds have passed and the day is old. The plough rusts and weathers.

When the harvest comes it is revealed again. The farmer wades to it and tilts it critically. It is hardly worth digging it out, taking it home in a cart and then on to the smithy. Time and the showers of summer have fused its coulter to its wedges, eaten the rim of the wheel worn thin by a thousand furrows. The old plough is dropped back into its bed in the weeds and the land takes it to its grave, a little slower than the chain harrows. A set of link harrows are in the mat of the turf root in a month. It needs a strong man to pull them away. If a horse is yoked to them the turf itself will come up as the horse drags them out. The fingers, or teeth, of the zigzag harrow dig into the ground. The weight of the frame carries them down when the rain has made the earth soft. The implements of thirty and forty years ago lie sleeping and quietly rusting away in the places that are so stony, rough and sour that no one wants to dig them out.

About the home pastures this thing happened now and again. The hard-worked implements that had seen better days were abandoned close to the places where they broke down. An old potato digger was held fast at the edge of one of the potato fields by the couch grass that had been piled there and left without being fired. In the stackyard an old binder sat sadly among the stacks. It was minus so many parts that it was hard to tell its mechanical features or its maker, but the sheet-iron bed sheltered many a laying-away hen, and fowls that were not rounded up from the stack butts at night perched up on the frame to roost, as safe there as anywhere, for they were hard to reach out on the struts of the broken flail or the rim of the seat.

Farmers are fond of bright paint on their carts and implements, when they are new. A cart is new just so long as the paint is bright orange and the name of the owner can be read on the plate, but how long is that? The bright new cart turns into the stable midden and comes out an old cart. The new binder sits a night or two in the field, waiting for cutting weather, and the shine is gone. This thing happened regularly. The best intentions in the world were forgotten when the wind was across a hill and the hill obscured in the mist of a cold rain. The old grubber stayed out there. The boy sent to cut weeds with a sickle could not reach the crop growing within the frame, and those weeds lived on to hide their protecting iron. It always fascinated me to see how a large implement began to look small when the weeds grew through it, about it and over it.

The plough was not always forgotten, however. Perhaps it had a feature that no other plough possessed.

'Boy, you'll take a horse to the back of the Big Hill. Up yonder, in the corner, you'll see a plough. It's been there a long time. Bring it down. It's the very thing for the Wee Five Acre. We'll get Adair to put a new sock on her and then sort out a set of chains. There's a swingletree in the cheese loft.'

Boy and horse went off to the back of the Big Hill. The plough was dragged from its hiding place. The cobwebs in the cheese loft were disturbed and the swingletree brought down. When I walked the hill with the gun I would stop at the place and see the imprint of the plough on the land, a bare patch, a few yellowed stalks of grass, a fringe of long grass that had grown up the ploughshare. Perhaps a mouse had lived in shelter here for a season. The beetles that had bred beneath the iron had scuttled away into the less friendly field. It took a little time before the exposed ground came to life, and then nature set about making it all good again.

Man can alter the drainage of a field, plant a hedge, put up a wall, dig a ditch and in a little while the ugliness of his work is camouflaged.

The verdure spreads and what he has done in a rough and ready way is screened first by quick-growing weeds, then by grass and finally, given time, by bushes and even trees. The pastures of home were gently threatened, year by year, by the encroaching gorse. Gorse hills were really outcrops of rock or stone heaps, but in time the gorse seeded and spread. A little round bush sat a little farther out in the field. The following year another took its place alongside the first. The field was reduced by three feet, the circumference of one bush, of two bushes, of three. Between the bushes the turf became finer because its roots thickened and matted. This turf the sheep would graze. The rabbits sported among the bushes on the fringe of the hill. Unchecked, a blackberry would spread there too. Soon the sheep could not penetrate and the area went back to the wild, growing those delicate harebells and feathery grasses.

I watched this thing happen year by year. The March Gate Field was left longer and longer without crop and the gorse hills grew larger and larger. I think I watched them with greater interest because the bigger they became the more rabbits sheltered in them. Partridges haunted the fringe, rabbits slept out there in the warm sun and hares were about quite often. The grand sight of a yellow gorse hill was a thing that made me wish I could paint. It was a place where I always wanted to take an afternoon nap. Indeed, I often did so. Grandfather expressed his displeasure at my 'sleeping in the whins' when there were so many useful tasks I might have been doing.

No matter how beautiful, no matter how fragrant the breath of the whin field, we were practical people. A day came when the gorse had to be halted. The outlying clumps were attacked with the whin hoe. The hills themselves were set on fire. Once or twice in summer now I get that wonderful breeze from the burning gorse. On the hilly farms behind the village they look at their pasture and decide the gorse must be set on fire. The smoke drifts down to us, a scent like no other, with all the nostalgic magic of peat smoke for me.

When we set fire to the gorse the smoke went into the heavens like the smoke from the sacrifice altar in the picture of the tabernacle in the wilderness that hung in one of the farmhouse bedrooms. The gorse glowed and crackled, the rabbits ran and the flames swept through, laying bare the stone heap, the rock and the charred sticks that were the thickest stems of the bushes. A torch was carried to the next and the one beyond that. The green and gold vanished and black and brown took their place. Here the hot earth smoked after the fire had died. No rabbit returned and the partridges did not come in again over the wall.

The scars remained. If the burning took place early in the year the recovery was quicker, but no matter when it happened the paintbrush of nature came sooner or later. The wind broke the charred sticks, the sheep pushed through them and on the ground the grass grew greener than it had been before. The stones, in wind and rain, the change from frost to mist, grew a coat of moss or grey lichen. The minute organism that was no more than a green slime developed on the face of the rock and became at length a crust of life, humus, dust, pollen and seed that clothed the naked stone. One summer and the black burn was hidden, two, and the young gorse was there again.

Hundreds of seeds mature and fall in such places, lacking the moisture, the air and the nourishment to come to mature life, but when the gorse bush is reduced by fire, somewhere under a cracked stone a seed survives. The crowding roots have died. There is space, there is air, and the soft rain of spring falls and the bush grows again. If this fails, the wind brings a seed over the dike or out from the hedge. The grass in the place where the old bushes were fired is not thick enough to deny the seed growing space. A thousand less fortunate seeds fall on the old-established turf without success. The wind blows them, the rain soaks them a score of times and they rot and die, but the seed that comes to the scorched earth germinates when the soil has recovered. The soil is enriched with new potash, new salts, and the young shoot thrives. For this reason the burning of gorse hills is an endless occupation, a thing to scent the summer air and make the basking rabbit run in frantic fear for the warren in the hedge.

The way to take gorse from a hill is with a mattock or whin hoe, to grub away the roots and break up the earth with a stout cultivator. In summer we had other things to do. When the thought came, someone went out and set fire to the whins. All the countryside knew it was being done. In the dim distance a man would halt in his field and put his hand to his eyes. They were burning whins out yonder, his thoughts would run. Now on what farm was it being done? The planting on the hill indicated it was near the Clutag March, below the Malzie Hill, above Hill-head, beyond Barness. The miles in between meant nothing. Old John employed Willie and Tam. He was hardly likely to send Tam on such a boy's job, so Willie, the dimwit, was burning the whins. Ah well, it was a pleasant thing to do when the sky was bright and the breeze rolling the blue smoke across the pasture. Oh, it was a pleasant job, and sometimes done out of sheer idleness on a Sunday when a man got tired sleeping his day away in the scent of the gorse bloom.

The wind that blows across the fields has an effect on them that makes their very character, for the wind brings more than rain in its path. It brings a dozen other things that have changed the land from the beginning of time. An old tree falls and leaves a gap in a hedge. The wind blows through the gap, altering the hedge and the field beyond. The tufts of grass begin to lean one way, as the hedge already leans. Look at the moss and lichen on the stones, growing to the north because the summer sun dries and kills growth that can withstand the coldest winter. Everything in the field reacts to the prevailing wind and the extent to which it is screened by a hill, a fence or a wall, or the rise and fall of the land itself.

Come up to the march of the moss and see the wind, for the wind can be seen. It flows towards us from somewhere out there, making a rippling sea of the fine grass, nodding the cotton heads, sleeking down the heather. The black, twisted tree on the boundary fence gives one of its leaves to the wind and a shower of small birds follow, like leaves themselves as they vanish over the curve of the hill. Look at the gorse on the edge of the peat bank, for it grows away from the wind. Its arms reach to the east, for the wind here is the old west wind, the wind of mist and rain when all the countryside is blanketed and hushed, and duck are flying in the dusk. Stand with me here at nightfall as I have often stood in this place. Even the moss rabbit bobs down the wind and the thistle that grows at the end of the fence has a natural curve in its stalk. Pick this stalwart weed and put it against the dock, and the curve in the stem would be the same, for the wind always blows in the same direction and plants that have lived the same length of time seem to lean away from it to the same degree. The old thorn does not lean. A thorn tree will not give an inch to a charging bull. It simply grows out of the wind, like the gorse.

This wind is the wind of autumn, a wind of speeding seed and flying leaf. The weeds have the wind to sow them, and the wind plucks away the head of the thistle, rattles the rusty dock, hammers the rat's tail against a stone until all the seeds are sown. If any are overlooked, tomorrow will find the finches in search of food and more will be carried away. Over the march fence, through the thorn and the gorse, up the brow and away above the hollow. What of the hollow? The wind down there is soft, a sort of undercurrent that ruffles the richer grass and shakes the rain out the briar. Here some of the seeds fall. In the spring they will rise in the black earth, carpeting the furrows where the potatoes are planted, crowding for life in the ryegrass. The wind-sown thistles will stand as they were sown, without pattern, mauve flowers above the fawn of the grass. Nor will the yellow weed be forgotten and the dock will grow too, thick and succulent, with only a touch of the rust of death on its leaves.

Here in the hollow, in the next field, the cattle will shelter. Walk down from the moss in the gloom of lowering night and you will find them along the hedge. The rain that sweeps over the hill sings among the hawthorn branches and steams on the backs of the black and white cows, but they are sheltered here, sharing the corner with a disconsolate horse that remembers the comfort of his stable, the warmth of a straw bed and the infrequent squeak of the rat hurrying across the rafters.

The stubble is bare, but the wind has left a mark on this field. The lying corn could not be lifted far enough to allow the binder or the reaper to crop it short and the straw rots on the field where the short

sheaves were gathered. Behind each dike that cuts across the wind the grass is thick and coarse, behind each little brow, and in the lee side of every shoulder, the soil is deeper, for the wind is old. It has blown the earth from a hundred little hills, changed the course of streams that have changed the course of rivers that have made seas.

A hedge is the life of a man. He plants his cuttings along a bank and watches them grow. In the life of his son it thickens and holds the wind from a field where crops improve. A long time ago a wood grew down the hollow behind the burn. The earth where it once grew is black and rich and no finer potatoes came from any soil than those lifted in this place. In the age when the wood fell and slumped into the earth on which it grew, the land that faced the wind must have changed so much that it is hard to picture it as it was. The bare slopes to the east that now feed a neighbour's sheep must have been green and rich. Now the sun scorches the grass and bakes it brown before the plover is gone. It is fit for sheep. The corn, when corn is grown, rises tall and proud, waves its green head, becomes ripe and weak in the back and folds to re-seed the furrow.

Across the arable land the wind streams and on through and over the stones of the dike. When it comes to the plain of the bog it sends waves across the round rushes and sets the reeds whispering. No tree grows and the bird that rises goes off into the east like the ball from a cannon. Never walk down this wind, for scent and sound go with it, but walk up the wind. The covey that feeds in the little islands of calm among the gorse cannot hear you coming. The pheasant will step out of the bracken before you, the hare will come leisurely to meet you and the sound of your shot be whipped away from the muzzle of your gun and carried across your shoulder, growing fainter and fainter, vanishing as the ripple of the rising trout vanishes in a pool. Walk up the wind when the pigeons are on the stooks of corn or in the trees of the wood. In the path of the wind they are deaf. They cannot hear your clumsy progress. They have only sight and you have the cover of the hedge, the wall. In the hedge the wind screams. It whistles through the wall.

Harvest in the fields kept everyone busy. My grandmother was a good housekeeper. Summer and autumn could not pass without blackberry and apple jelly being made, blackberry wine brewed, mushroom ketchup boiled and strained. A dozen other tasks were done. The blackcurrants were gathered, the apples from the ancient apple trees. Some things could be relied upon, but the mushrooms depended on the season. A warm sun, a misty evening, that combination of heat and dampness that makes the

spawn active in the old turf, and the mushroom crop was there. It came in some distant field, in the sheltered hollow. Often, although mushrooms were expected, the signs were missed. Crossing a neighbour's field a week later, the growth would be discovered and my aunts would return with the bad news.

'In the hollow yonder, a basket of them, but every one had the worm in it! Such a pity. The ketchup your grannie could have made!'

Grandmother was always ready to cope with the unexpected. A morning dawned and there they were, covering the Sow's Field, as lovely as anything that grows, button mushrooms of one size and another, differing in an hour's growth. I remember going out and helping to lift them with two large egg baskets. The field yielded sacks of mushrooms. A secret that only the old turf knew had come to light. The crop never came again, to my knowledge. We carried them to the house, where they were sorted and stalked, boiled up with the spicy things that went to make the black ketchup, strained and left to cool. The straining darkened the fingers of those who had this job. The ketchup swam on our plates for a while, making the floury potatoes black, and then we tired of surfeit and used it as it was meant to be used, but oh, the flavour of the fungus, the flavour of autumn as wonderful as the first glass of matured blackberry wine, the first spoonful of jelly from the great brass pan!

Because the taste for ketchup was a family weakness, all mushrooms gathered were saved for this purpose, one bottle being made when the supply would run to no more.

Grandfather would lift the bottle and help himself.

'I'll have no more of this,' he would say. 'It gives me the damnedest heartburn!'

I think he had the damnedest heartburn all his days, or at least while my grandmother lived, for I never noticed the bottle at the other end of the table without its being passed to him and used as it was always used.

Years later, when ketchup was not made, I went out into the Wee Field and found a cluster of mushrooms, those snow-white and flesh-pink mushrooms that grow on the cleanest fields. I picked them and hurried back, deciding to have my breakfast there and then instead of going off with the gun.

'Could I have them fried or stewed, please?' I asked.

'Are they nice like that?' my aunts asked together.

Grandmother had been a maker of ketchup such as no one else could make. Her daughters had not tried to equal her, and it had never entered their heads to put the mushrooms to any other use. They had never tasted fried or stewed mushrooms. I think they had a secret feeling that there was something wrong in cooking them in this way. I had my breakfast, fried mushrooms as rich as liver. Each morning I looked in likely places for more, but I found more puffballs than mushrooms, and soon the frost was across the grass and no more fungus grew. The puffballs shrank and went to dust, the fairy rings yellowed and vanished as even fleshy toadstools vanish when the cold weather sets in. I have had ketchup since, but no one can get the flavour of the ketchup we had when I was a boy.

Above the quarry stood two trees, both of them old trees. Once they had looked down on a small farm. In those far-off days they could have been no more than ash poles. Perhaps the old gooseberry bushes in the hollow had had heavy crops, but, as the trees grew and matured, the bushes declined. How long does a gooseberry bush live? Its wood becomes tough and strong as blackthorn. The leaves get smaller and the fruit loses size every year. When I first knew the quarry hollow the gooseberry bushes were on a little island round which the bog was spreading. The fruit was small. It ripened to a golden shade. The berries were hairy, but when I ate a few I discovered that they were sweet. The bushes never had enough fruit to satisfy. I had to be content with a handful.

Time passed and a fungus took the heart out of one of the ash trees and the berries on the gooseberry bushes were fewer and fewer each season. The decline in this corner went with the spread of the bog. The evening air was perfumed by the scent of the myrtle that grew in the black earth, the footprints of waterfowl marked the mud. The ash trees were both becoming hollow. Once I saw a rabbit take shelter in the hollow trunk of one and a dog thrust his head in after it as far as he could. The tree was little more than a shell at ground level. I called the dog off and found the rabbit had squeezed into one of the hollow roots. It was a nice young buck in fine condition and I took it home for the pot.

An ash tree that is dying provides little shelter from the wind and less shade for a beast escaping from the sun. These two trees made a fine lookout for the pigeons raiding the cornfield. A great flock of birds would come raggedly round and alight on the top branches. They could see a long way before they decided to go down and often one of their number remained there as sentry. I mentioned this at home when I brought a brace of birds back from the stubble one evening.

'The two trees have been there as long as I can remember,' said grandfather, 'but even trees come to old age. We'll have them down.'

We looked out axes, a crosscut saw, some rope and a crowbar. It was a grand adventure. Have you ever set about cutting down a tall dead tree with a trunk that time has made as hard as iron? Lumbermen will smile. The tallest tree will yield to the axe in a matter of minutes provided the man with the axe has experience. A crosscut saw will rip through a trunk three or four feet in diameter in not much more time than a man takes to sit down and have a cigarette. We had no skill with axe or saw. Once a year we went to the fir planting to cut fence poles and stack props, but that was the extent of our ability. The crosscut seemed as blunt as the axe when put to the task and yet the axe had an edge to make me shiver. A few chips scattered over the turf. The bare old ash did not quiver or shake. A little lichen fell from its trunk. That was all. The crosscut rasped away and made a trickle of sawdust. My hands became blistered with the axe. The saw made my back tired. The tree grew taller

each time I looked at its dead top.

They had a habit of making disparaging remarks about effort when they brought the afternoon tea to the field.

'Not so fit this afternoon?' the tea-bringer would ask. 'Five row lifted in a whole afternoon?' or 'Did the plough break and have to be mended?'

The tea came and the disparagement with it.

'You boys had better wait until the wind blows it down. It looks strong enough to stand for years yet! Grandfather was up the old road. He said it was likely you were sleeping behind the dike, for he could still see the top of the tree.'

It was true. The top of the ash trees at the quarry could be seen from the steading. Our failure to put even one of them on the grass was apparent to those at home. We put new power to the crosscut as the tea things were taken back. Late in the afternoon we were three-quarters of the way through that trunk. It was hollow, but the shell was of steel. At last, when the tree locked on the saw and the axe became blunt, I climbed up the trunk and fastened a rope to a branch. The tugs we gave made the tree sway a little. Pull after pull made it begin to rock. Once we had it rocking we knew it would come down. We tugged and gasped, gasped and tugged, and the tree gave a loud crack, groaned and came crashing down. I fell over backwards to avoid some of the branches. The sound of its falling was heard at home, for it crashed on the dike and brought down six or seven yards of stones. We stood dismayed looking at the havoc we had wrought. Grandfather came over the hill, plodding steadily with his walking stick. He said nothing until he was among us.

'Godsake,' he scolded. 'I asked you to bring down the tree and you knock the devil out of the dike. Tomorrow you can saw up the trunk, clear it away, and build up the stones again. If you'd set about the thing in the right way you'd have had the tree lying downhill!'

We were too tired to say anything. The prospect of cutting up the tree was too awful to be contemplated. In the morning we went sadly down to the quarry and began to cut the tree into logs. We cut from the tip first because the cutting was easier. When we had enough cleared we roped the trunk and dragged it down the slope. The building of the drystone wall was a pleasure. The other ash tree? It stands there yet, as far as I know. The pigeons will still glide round and settle in its withered, bald arms. When it comes down it will surely be the gale that brings it down. Time changed this corner, spread the bog, grew grass in the bowl of the quarry and made the gooseberries small. Time will bring down the old ash.

The quarry was no more than eight feet deep. It was cut into the rock of the hill. Cattle had a habit of standing on the brink. Sheep often scampered down into the shelter of the bowl. It was not often used, but once in a while a cart was sent down and a load of stone taken for making up the road. The road to the march gate was full of potholes. The creamery cart, a spring cart to give it its right name, jolted and bounced through these holes with such violence that sometimes the lids came off the cans. When milk was lost it followed that the time had come to make up the road, and the old quarry was visited.

No stone hammer was needed in the quarry. The rock was rotten. It broke into layers that were blue and dusty red in colour. They could be quickly loaded by hand. The face from which they were pulled sagged and the red earth crumbled down. In a few showers the place looked as it had always looked. The grass spread among the fragments of rock and a gorse bush took root, for gorse will root among the rocks and on the poorest soil. I remember finding a pheasant there in the summer and putting up a cock and several hens from the gorse in early winter. One of the birds fell close to the stump of the old ash tree and the other dropped in the bog. I got a black leg scrambling after it. The bog embraced me as it had done more than once when on a wet night I tried to recover a duck. The fine cock bird lay as he had fallen, making a sort of hollow for himself on the soft weed. I got him and laid him beside the hen. When birds are split up they usually leave the locality, but a week later I shot another hen in the same place. I think they found it warm and sheltered there, and they had only to fly up out of the quarry, cross the dike, to be in the stubble where they could still make a gleaning of oat ears that had fallen in the summer.

It is strange how the place where man has made his home holds something after he has ceased to live there. I have noticed this thing about derelict country cottages, abandoned farmsteads in the Welsh hills, and there are hundreds of them. At the quarry there was no sign that there had ever been a farm on the spot, or, as grandfather insisted, a bit of a village, a clachan, as we call it in the north. High up on the hill there stood the gable of a cottage, part of a dike now, but down at the quarry I searched for the foundations of the cottages of the clachan. They had been ploughed out, carried away to stone heaps or buried in the bog as it came slowly up the hollow.

The gooseberry bushes were the only sign that man had ever been there, and I wondered whether the bushes had not been seeded there by a bird. I could even imagine some toiler throwing away his scone spread with gooseberry jam, or his piece of gooseberry tart, and thereby sowing the bushes in the place. Yet, when I stood in the hollow, looking up at the ash tree and the thorn on the other side of the burn, I knew it was a friendly place, a place with the associations of man, his stone-walled cottage, his smoke-blackened chimney stack, peat burning on his hearth and the gooseberry bushes heavy with ripe fruit.

The hollow was not big. It opened on to the bog, but it was sheltered from the wind from the west and south-west. At its narrow top, the land came round and made a barrier against the north. Looking down it I faced the morning sun. I loved to go there early, when the frost was still on the field. Across the wall in the bog field a hare often came up, hopping across the ploughing, going on towards the gap that led to the Wee Five Acre and the Switchback Hill. I did not always take a shot there. I liked to look round this place and imagine the long-dead people coming out of their little stone houses and glancing at the sunrise, red and gold beyond the bog and the far hills.

The stackyard has something of all the fields in it, for the harvest of hay and corn has brought every weed and herb from the fields. The seeds have fallen from the carts, blown away when the hay was taken for fodder, or dropped through the riddles and sieves of the mill. On the unused rick-butts vetch grows among the stones. When the season is wet, charlock is there with tall sorrel, hardheads, dock. The oats have seeded, and the special mixture that was sown for the first time in the hayfield last season has spread its hardier specimens in the turf between the ricks and the drystone wall. There is something hopeful about this accidental reproduction. If harvests failed, or crops were lost through fire or flood, a handful of oats could be gathered in some quiet corner and saved and nursed as the first crops were saved and nursed by the man who made a cultivating tool of his spear.

The oats grow as conditions in the rickyard permit. Here, there is no harrowing and rolling. The soil is not fertilised, save by the decaying grass and straw. The seeds among the stones and weeds are slow to germinate, slow to shoot. They are at the mercy of the straying fowl from the farmyard, the grass-hungry goose, the duck that searches the rank growth for the slug that hides in the damp roots. When it grows out of the undergrowth it is green and strong because it is not crowded by a million other blades of its kind. Its green shade always reminded me of the corn in Hiawatha. It grew alone, swayed by the wind, watered by a score of summer downpours and ripened when the crop from the field was already in the stack. Sometimes its life was cut short, for the stackyard ran low, the straw stack was demolished, the last hay and the last corn long since consumed, and when this happened no one bothered to make sure the gate was properly fastened. The stackyard became the rooting place of the sows. They ripped up the turf by the yard, cropped the stately corn before its time, and left nothing but a nettlebed where a black Minorca went to lay each afternoon.

There is no time that brings more satisfaction to a farmer's heart than the day he can stand and look at his rickyard, knowing that the barrel stacks are well thatched and dry, that every straw is off the stubble and the year's work a tangible thing at last, so many stacks, so many bushels, so many bales.

An old stackyard has its own life. The drystone wall shelters a rat or two, even when the butts are empty. The field mouse lives in the long

grass and among the weeds, for all the chaff heaps that are mouldering have a little grain among them. The vole is there too. He may make a nest in the soft earth at the far end, risking his life to be there, for the weasel or the stoat knows that where the grain is stored there is always food.

The harvest comes in, and with it a token of the life of the field. In the hayfield the fork plunges into a coil of hay and swings it to the cart before the shrew or the field mouse can escape. Once in a while even an adder is transported. Many a toad and several frogs may come too. The haystack is warm. In its first days it is hot, and then it settles. The clover shrivels, the flowers of the field and all the scented grasses give off that wonderful breath that is hay. The shrew ventures to run back to the pasture and learns that a cat will sit all afternoon like a statue, waiting for that very moment. The field mouse adapts himself and makes his runs and tunnels where the weight of hay will allow. He runs beneath the ropes on the roof of the stack, an inch beneath the round rush thatch. The cat learns to wait for him there. The owl sails round the stack and alights to grab his prey when the mouse is foolish enough to expose himself. Even a mouse likes to be out in the free, fresh air of a summer night. He cannot stay forever below the thatch, in the shelter of a wall or behind a wainscot. The pattern of things first made the mouse and helpless creatures of his kind, the vole, the hedgehog, the shrew, the beetle and a thousand others, begin to seek their food when darkness was on the land. The creatures which depended on them for their food began to hunt at night, developing that uncanny power to make day of night.

When the corn crop is in, the grey rat moves from the stones of the wall to the corn stack. All the other inhabitants of the stackyard are harmless, but the rat is an unhealthy, filthy wretch. He tunnels through the stack, making chaff of the oats, leaving his galleries mildewed and stale as he goes on and on. He is safe from the cat. The owl does not often surprise him on the thatch. It is when the threshing mill arrives that he finds his day has come. The stack is ringed with wire netting. Three or four dogs are waiting for him, half a dozen pitchforks, a few heavy cudgels. The slaughter is fast and furious when the last sheaves are forked to the mill. One escapes under the wire unnoticed, another crouches among the stones and the dogs fail to find him. When the sound of the mill has ceased to echo from the hill and dusk is settling about the place, these rats go scurrying off in search of new shelter. They move by fits and starts, as cautious and cunning as any of their kind.

Watch the rat on the grass verge, close to the cart track. He sits sniffing the night air, no more than a shadow, a small boulder. His first dash takes him ten or fifteen feet along the track. Now he crouches by the chickweed and groundsel, listening to the night, the faraway squeaks and squeals of his kind. When he is sure it is safe to cross the road, he darts across and once again blends with the shadows in the deeper gloom. He cannot hear the hushed wings of the owl, but every sense is alert. Perhaps even the whisping to and fro of his relative, the bat, makes his heart beat faster. He is on a journey to some safer home and, although he is moving at night, every yard is an adventure. If the owl comes he must dart to cover, into the weeds, through the black forest of the nettle bed, along the wall, and on the wall a cat may be sitting, waiting for his supper to come to him.

Everyone who has seen a cat hunting knows his way. He sits very still, tenses, springs, and, if he fails, makes a tender-footed run to the place where his quarry has taken refuge. The rat knows the way of the cat and the owl. Both strike once. Their second effort hardly ever succeeds, but the first strike – the first strike is the thing that puts that nervous twitch in the whiskers of rat and mouse.

This stackyard rat we were watching runs into the shadow of the stable wall. He is making a sort of reconnaissance. Under a door by way of a drain he goes, through a dark, warm place with a cobbled floor and a hundred dusty cobwebs. He runs and stops, runs and stops, and each time he stops he listens. The pigeon in the wood lives and preserves himself in much the same way. He coos and pauses, listens, coos again and listens once more. Let one stick crack, one stone fall from the wall in that interval, and he will be off.

The rat will find cover behind the corn chest, under the door, among the straw, anywhere, in ten seconds or less, if the straw rustles, a cat mews, a moth flutters against the grimy windows. If he finds no place where he can feed on bran or corn, if all the troughs in the stable are clean, all the granary and barn doors firmly fastened and reinforced with sheet iron, he will go out once more to try his luck in the open. Often, encountering no others of his kind, he will take to the fields. Rats come and go in a strange way. One year, when food is plentiful and doors and walls in a bad state of repair, the rats will arrive, undermine the barn flags, tunnel and bore through walls, scurry through the pig houses and every loft and attic corner. Some strange happening will take them away again. They will disappear almost overnight.

The grey rat that takes to the field will not be long in the wild. A day or two he may frequent a hedge or a bank, but his life in the shelter of farm walls, where food is plentiful, makes him ill-equipped for the open. He is too fat at first and in continual danger because he has no home. His quarters are temporary ones, the first at hand and without natural defence. The stoat can come upon him day or night. The owl is oftener in the hedge than along the stackyard wall. Soon he makes his way on, seeking the comfort he finds in the dwellings of man. Man may put down a cage trap or a bait, but he is in no great danger unless all other food is hidden away in safe places. When he runs the last few yards to a new steading, he knows that he is home where he belongs, a parasite, a spoiler of stored grain, a ripper of sacks, a robber of feed trays and troughs.

The owl that hunts the stackyard thatch takes a mouse and sails away carrying the little thing in its claws. Once in a while he drops into the weeds and seizes the round, furry vole. By the burn he gets a water vole in that tense moment before the vole throws himself into the water. It is only when the harvest is threshed that the bleary-eyed grey rat gets his deserts. He dies fighting desperately, getting no mercy, showing none.

If the corncrake calls, summer is young and the oats half-grown. To go in search of him is to chase the rainbow, seek the water shrew or find the cuckoo's egg. The corncrake belongs to the elusive world of animals and birds. It is hard to see and identify the water shrew, for he flits across the pool like a brown shadow, a dead leaf pulled by an invisible thread. The crake calls and the man in the hollow looks up and listens. It is a sound that the busy world does not know. Fewer and fewer are the numbers of those who have heard it and hear it yet. Indeed, I have not heard the

corncrake myself for many summers. It is eight or nine years since I saw him here in Wales.

In those days there were fewer tractors. The hill farms were quiet. Horses still pulled the roller and the reaper. I walked uphill along the side of a wood. The corn was half ripe and yet not tall, for it was growing on poor ground. The crake rose at my feet, flew ahead and settled on a bare patch. I watched him. He darted forward through some thistles and went on among stunted gorse to the hedge bottom. I stood long after he was gone, fixing every detail in my mind. I am not a bird watcher in the strict sense. I knew that this experience might not come again, because the bird was rare already. I did not hear the call in the locality either before I saw the crake or after, and I have wondered since whether the corncrake can breed in a place and not be heard. Perhaps not. The thought is a pleasant one, a fancy that makes the extermination of the land rail kind less definite.

When the fields of home were one third under the plough every year, and two thirds of the ploughing seeded in corn, the crake was often there. The call is old. Somehow it suggests to me a scene of agriculture as it was when the harvest came down to the scythe and was threshed with a flail on a winnowing floor. I think of it now and remember the summer evening with the air almost still, the peat smoke going up from the kitchen chimney, the midges beneath the branches of the apple trees in the garden down the road, and the footpath below the stile perfumed with the scent of honeysuckle that twined so thickly in the thorn hedge that the trees were strangled.

The first time I ever heard it I was told that it was the corncrake. No one thought anything of the fact. The crakes came every year. They were out there in the old road field, in the Barness Field, the Big Hill, the Switchback Hill. The call was hardly more remarkable than the call of the partridge. The partridge call meant that a covey was being reared in one of the nearby fields. The corncrake would not make a supper when September came. The sound had no special significance any more than had the purring of the nightjar.

Time passed and the crake came not so often. Grandfather remarked on its absence. Once I went in search of it in a great field of hay. The field belonged to a neighbour. The crake was there. I could tell where the bird was within two hundred yards. I began to walk through the hay towards it and the sound died. Perhaps I passed within inches of the nest. I did not know the habits of the ground birds so well in those days. The call died and a breeze ran across the field. The evening light seemed to fall and all at once I felt lonely. From a long way away someone whistled me out of the hay. I was doing a senseless thing, walking after a will-o'-the-wisp and breaking the stalks with my stumbling feet.

If you see the corncrake you will remember him, for he is a strange little chopped-off sort of bird. In a way, he has the build of an immature thrush, but his colouring is rich, a rich brown, chestnut, a stripe of blue-grey on the head, bars on its sides. It is a nervous, inconspicuous bird in its movements. Its neck shoots out when it is startled and when it flies its legs hang behind it as the legs of a waterhen are trailed when the bird takes off. Once, I confess now with real shame, I shot a corncrake. When I had a gun in my hand and a great urge to use it, I went round the farm morning and afternoon as well as evening. My brother went with me as often as not. I was rather proud of the keenness of my eye, the way I could throw up the gun and make a pheasant or partridge spin out of its flight. I would shoot the moment a target presented itself and many a bird was ruined.

We were walking through the bog, looking for a hare, when the crake rose. It sprang up from my feet, an unusual thing for such a bird to do when there was so much cover. It had gone about twenty-five yards when I shot it. At the moment the bird was hit I knew I had made a mistake. We could not claim a partridge, pheasant, snipe, woodcock or anything I had ever shot before. I picked it up and looked at it. I knew the corncrake as I had never known it before. I discovered that it had a short beak, the colour of a game bird, the frame of the waterhen, the water rail. I knew it was a thin, poor little creature. I looked at my brother. He was not admiring my marksmanship but beginning to think that my hand and eye were too quick. I took the bird home. Grandfather was away. My aunts had never heard of anyone shooting a corncrake, let alone eating one. The carcass was shamefully consigned to the midden. I had helped to contribute to the extermination of the species.

The corncrake nests in the long grass, among the growing hay, in the fringe of the oatfield. The nest is not unlike the nest of the partridge and the eggs are pale yellow, buff, flecked with brown. I have found the nest twice, seen the bird four or five times in my life, heard the cry, like others who know the crake, a few score times. It is a thing a man enjoys knowing he has seen and heard. I enjoy it the way I enjoy the thought that I have held the water shrew in my hand, found the nest of the nightjar and have seen a snake devouring a toad.

When I think of the birds of the pasture I think of the starlings that came to the hole in the gable above the pig house. The starling pair is one of a thousand that go singing and shrilling over the fields to alight among the grazing sheep. The signs of the starlings among the sheep make the shepherd send his dog to bring down the flock, because the scavengers are either picking the maggot, the maggot sore, or soiling the sheep and sowing the larva of the fly. The starling kind are dirty, flea-ridden creatures. Their lime burns the wood and destroys the growing

tree. When the morning sun is on the roof, the starling perches on the highest point and begins to sing. The feathers of his throat ruffle with the delight of song. While he sings he is in ecstasy. The day comes when the brood is hatched. The parents go to and fro bringing food every minute.

The nest, made of every straw, every piece of wool, every fragment they could find, becomes fouled and sour. The blood-sucking ticks breed. The clamouring brood grows and becomes more cramped than the magpie family. They fly into the pasture and learn to feed across the dewy turf.

The sheep are brought in, looked over, and set on the road to the dipping pens. The starlings go murmuring across the land, bustling among each other, rising, swinging round and settling, quarrelling and feeding. In ten minutes they have crossed the field. At the hedge they rise and cross into the next field. The sun shines, noon comes and goes, and they are five miles from the field where the sheep were grazing. Walk up the dikeside, and they will rise and hurry off with a great flurry of wings. They drop two fields away and begin that endless walk that takes them from one side of the country to the other. In winter they crowd in one tree, murmuring until night settles. The tree roots die because the lime bites the bark and burns the ground at the roots.

In spring a pair of birds with all the sheen of healthy plumage on them settle on the ridge of the byre. Soon they are driving the sparrow from his hole beneath the rainpipe cleats. The robbers have returned. Impudence across the grass, feeding at the heels of the cattle. The birds that live in holes in trees are driven out to make room for the couples that come to the wood. The nuthatch loses his home, the woodpecker finds them in possession. When they have done with the fresh hole it is fit for no other bird. The black and grey, glossy birds lay a clutch of blue eggs and work feverishly bringing up their young. The food they bring includes everything that can be found on a field, every bug and weevil, every grub and worm. The farmer would not have them rise from his pasture. He likes to see them there, even among the sheep.

I remember a pair of starlings coming to nest in the chimney of the farmhouse. Grandfather believed that it was a lucky house in which a bird nested. He was reluctant to move a bird, even the barn owl that reared her young a few yards from his bed. These starlings had the same habit as the jackdaw. They brought in enough to make a comfortable nest, and a comfortable nest is one which fills the space. They brought in a hundredweight of rubbish, strands of grassrope, bits of twig, fibres, grass, feathers. The material filled a barrow and the noise of the nest-builders heralded the rising sun. When the first lot was taken away they began on a second building. In the end I shot them. Everyone was pleased except grandfather. I could not persuade him that their fleas might spread from the chimney to the bedroom. Even when the birds were dead, he insisted I had brought bad luck on the place. Later I shot one of the owls that kept the family from sleeping, wheezing away on the gable throughout the night. I don't think I was ever completely forgiven for these crimes.

You have permission to shoot in these fields. You know them well, for you have been round them with me more than once. You know their life, the streams that flow through them, every sheltering hedge and wood, every peat bank, every gorse hill, every spring. Come when you will, except on the Sabbath when one of the family takes his nap in the parlour, another dozes in the attic bedroom, and another in the armchair by the window, while a fourth or fifth goes off to 'show face' at the kirk. Come in the hour before twilight, the hour after dawn, come on the day when the frost is stiffening the mud at the gate to the bog, or when the sun is glittering in the march gate pool. So long as the family knows you and can recognise your figure crossing the hill, you have freedom to shoot when and where you like. You must remember the marches. You must not knock too many stones from the dike, or fall foul of neighbours or keepers. Whatever the law about protected birds, you must not shoot the peewit, the owl. You can have your cursed curlew if you wish, for we have Covenanter blood in us, and no affection for the cry that betrayed so many good men. Because we hate nothing so much as high-handed authority, you may knock over a pheasant before the keeper's nose, if you can get away with it. Give him a run for his money.

Come in the morning and see the place as it is when day comes up from behind the rise that is the Sow's Field and the three elms standing black to the grey of the sky. The march gate chain is cold to the hand.

The links jangle. The water of the puddle in the road is discoloured by the disturbed mud. Your feet are on the rough stones that came from the old quarry, and ahead is the blackness of the garden hedge, trimmed hawthorn screening the apple trees and the bare trunks of the heaven-reaching pines. You can see the steading in the half-light, the whitewashed walls, the pump and the trough on the gable walk. The windows are asleep. The house sleeps still. No trickle of smoke comes from the blackened chimney. It's half an hour before they will be down, fanning the embers of the old fire with a folded newspaper, putting on shoes, searching for aprons, hurrying to get ready for the milking while one sets herself with determination to the making of a cup of tea. The dog hears you pass and cocks his ears. He knows from your step that you are not sneaking to the chicken run or stealing to the barn door.

There are two ways of going round the place, clockwise and anti-clockwise. Habit, the position of the sun, the prevailing wind or breeze, make most people go against the clock, into the sun. Turn now and cut through into the Wee Field. Look to your gun, see that it is cocked and that the sleep is brushed from your eyes. Often on this morning journey I was halfway across the Wee Field before I was awake. Sometimes it took me five minutes to leap out of bed, dress, put on my boots, pick up my gun and leave the house. Many a time I only awoke when my nerves were shocked by the first shot I fired. That shot was often in the Wee Field. Often it did better work than the alarm set to get the milkers out of bed.

The rabbits that feed along the hedge of the Wee Field are wary creatures. They are used to someone popping across to get something for the pot. They run when the fence squeals as you cross it, or at the little groan of the wicket gate's hinges. The mist of morning is in the Wee Field. It obscures the shadowy movement of the rabbits that speed for the hedge. You have no chance. Walk down the hedge, keeping close to the gorse bushes and the briar tangles. If there is nothing in the Wee Field you may get a shot across the bank into the March Gate Field. Remember you can be seen from the Other Clutag Hill, from the gorse hills of the March

Gate Field, from the brow that stands above the waterhole. The rabbits feeding along the ditch hop gently into cover as you approach. You could shoot one that sits up on the bank, but he is close to his burrow. Another that you had not noticed bumps out of a patch of feathery grass and vanishes into the warren, but step gently and slowly. Two more sit out there in the dewy tufts. They must run soon. Be ready, for the time has come. They run with all the speed they have. The gun comes up, the shot echoes in the hill and the second barrel follows. Far off the rooks turn in flight, a shower of starlings change their course, and at home the dog, waiting to bark the herd to the byre, cocks his head intelligently and turns to look at the mist on the Other Clutag Hill.

Run man, run! Your first shot turned the rabbit head over heels. His mate is escaping to the burrow, for your shot was late and broke its back legs. In a minute she will have scrambled, crawled, dragged her damaged body to the hole. You must stop her, for her death will be slow and cruel. Grab her before the grass covers the last sight of her. Bring her out and crack her in the back of the neck with a side cut of your palm.

Because you are idle and thought little before you came, you have either to carry these two rabbits in your hand and manage the gun as well as you can, or leave them here. If you leave them, the hunting cat or a vagrant dog may come upon them before you return, unless you splice their legs and hang them in the tree. Now they are hung out of harm's way you can take your time. The shot went off on the breeze of the morning, but round the hill the rabbit tribe went to cover. Take your time. The next shot will be over the moss fence or across the moss dike at the edge of the little planting. Walk slowly. Give the world time to steady

its fast-beating heart. Stand and stare across the moss and fill your lungs with that wonderful air, that intoxicating freshness of the new day. There is nothing in life like it, this scent of gorse, this fragrance of the herbs and plants of the peat banks, the cool air that does something to the blood and caresses the cheek.

In the moss, a trickle of mist runs away on the breeze. The water among the distant round rushes is cold. You can imagine the snipe that feed there. Your eagerness brings the cackle of the grouse to your ear, but it did not happen. It did not happen. No painted mallard drake rose and turned to show his beauty in the brightening light. Only a small bird, a twite, a finch, went undulating across the waste, making a happy, sharp little twitter as it went. Yonder, below the far dike, a tall hare moves. Stand still and watch. Life was made for just this. Time is nothing but the running down of clock weights and the swing of a pendulum, but here is life, the hare crossing the moss in the silence and beauty of morning when the first milk cart is still unyoked, the first fires scarcely drawing enough to make smoke above a chimney. The whole thing is too wonderful to be disturbed by man or the unholy sound of his gun. All the world was once like this, a wild thing moving in a wilderness and a hunter watching it from the shelter of a tree. The man watching had no powder and lead and he was content. When he got his powder and lead he came out of the wilderness and found he had to use them on his neighbour.

The hare has gone. The old moss rabbit bobs halfway across the moss. One of his brown brothers appears closer at hand. The moss is riddled with holes, sleeping-places, false burrows that help a fleeing rabbit to throw off his pursuer. This one comes in towards you, not fast, but with purpose. He is coming to the fence to cross to the sweeter grass. His run is plain across the short grass on the first peat bank. He comes, forty-five yards, forty yards, thirty-five yards, over a lump, down a hollow and on. Shoot him now. The curlew rises out there. A hare that was in the reedy grass before the rushes bolts for his life, and a bird goes out of the rowan tree along the fence there. The rabbit dies in his tracks.

Now the Little Planting has echoed the shot. Everything along the planting's edge has taken cover. You can walk steadily on, over the ditch, across the end of the planting, up the hollow by the planting's side to the far march of the Little Planting Hill. Across the march wall, if you stand long against the background of the tall gorse you may get another shot. Listen to the Little Planting, to the sighing of the arms of pine and fir, to the sad rustle of the sycamore leaf, the flutter of the ash. No pigeon calls. The morning is suddenly old, although the sun is deep behind the hill and the day has not warmed the rough field or the moss.

There is nothing to be had here. Follow the march wall, on up the back of the Little Planting Hill to the high wood. In the side of the thorn hedge that runs to the high wood a rabbit runs, but it is too far ahead. Hold your fire. Some men would put up a gun at a gnat, try to shoot a bird half a mile away, but if you want to shoot well, calm yourself, swing smoothly, take your weight on your left foot, be comfortable in your old coat, shoot with deliberation, keep both eyes open, look at your bird. There are three kinds of men using guns. One is a natural shot. He could not tell you what he does. He puts up his gun and shoots, that is all. Somehow, every time he does it the bird begins to fall. An old Welsh farmer I know has this gift. He does not shoot often. He suffers badly with a chest complaint. I am sure no one ever bothered to give him a lesson in his life. No doubt he was sent out to scare birds when he was ten or twelve, but he shoots with a sureness that many a great game shot would envy. The other kinds of shot are the man who controls himself and makes the best of what little talent and coordination he has, and the man who simply does not shoot in the sense of shooting, but pulls the trigger and points his barrel in the general direction, often in that order, and to the terror of those who are with him.

We were on the Low Planting Hill, coming along the hedge on the high wood march. At the corner of the high wood you may pause and take a breather on the dike. It is a good thing to do, to look at morning in a wood, to see the breeze among the bracken, to feel the coldness of the stones and know that it is grand to be alive in such a place. You could shoot for the pot here. Along the dike a young rabbit, oblivious of your presence, hops out from a hole through the stones, enters the nettles and appears on the hay stubble. He nibbles at the clover, looks round, rears on his back legs, lowers himself and scratches himself with a hind foot. Like the hare in the moss, he must live. He is part of the magic, unaware and helpless.

Cross the end of the high wood, climb the wall and go down the dip of the Switchback Hill. Across these hills you walk for the pleasure of being on them, for all the world can see you here. The rabbits in the hollow down the side of the high wood and the pigeons in the tops of the trees can see you plainly. Now you are on the second part of the Switchback, going down to the farthest corner of the farm, where stunted bracken grows on the face of the hill among little clumps of blackberry. The soil here is thin. There is work for the whin hoe. A rabbit sleeps in one of these little round bushes of gorse. He is out behind us and bouncing away before we catch sight of him. Try a shot now as he runs on the very perimeter of the hill, snap at him before he is in cover. Did he fall or did he run on? The hill takes a little of the breath away. You pant up and across to the place where you think he was at the moment you fired. No? Perhaps not. An uphill shot at such an angle and with so little target is hard, but have you looked well? There he lies, five yards ahead, without a kick or a twitch in his body.

Every time you do this thing you disturb the birds for a mile. How many hares have left this big field while our feet have plodded up and down? Only the bracken, the gorse and the frail brown grass could tell.

Along the bottom of the Switchback Hill we go, past the solitary thorn, knee-deep in bracken. It is strange how, even after a shot has been fired, a rabbit still hides out in a field. The inclination to wait until the last minute is strong in the rabbit. Some fear or nervous hesitation will keep one or two crouching in the grass, making use of their natural camouflage, holding on until it is too late. Another rises above us, but we let him go, for we are near the Wee Five Acre and we have thoughts of game. Step over the broken wall and go first to the bottom corner.

Pheasants seem less inclined to run uphill and rise, but give them a start on a downhill stretch and they run at once, reach the boundary and launch themselves into the air before you are in range. Halfway to the bottom you see the hen running for the ditch. Steady. She is only one. There are others to left and right of us. In two strides or three, the air will be filled with the clatter and racketing of rising birds, and you have to use this gun as it was designed to be used, left and right.

The men who kill left and right are men who have control. They take a shot calmly, turn from a certain hit, make a new swing and shoot again. Once I shot a hare with my right barrel and a cock pheasant with the left, another time I shot a rising pheasant and a partridge that rose in a covey at the same moment. I can remember shooting a pair of pigeons, one coming and the other turning away, as high as any shot I have ever made. In spite of this, I do not think I was ever a good shot. My heart beat too fast. I anticipated the moment too often. It was only when I controlled myself and lost a little of the thrill that I was able to shoot cleanly and well.

The birds are in the air and flying for the hedge. While they were on the ground they took direction, downhill, over the hedge and out of sight in the shelter of the bog. Your two shots crash out and a cock bird towers above the hedge and falls back into the ditch. A hen thumps on to the ground on the other side, but you cannot be sure that this second bird is lying in the place where she fell. She may be back on her feet running for the rushes. A winged pheasant can cover a great distance in a short time. Scramble over the ditch and break through. The field is bare. The hen is gone. The rushes are motionless. Every second takes her farther in to the protecting forest. You have no hope of finding her without a good dog, a springer, a cocker, a Labrador retriever. Without the dog you must be content with the cock that lies in the ditch.

The turnip leaves are fluttering in the breeze. Walk the field now and the partridge covey that was frantically working its way across the furrows, putting as much distance between us as it could, shoots out over the low dike to the Switchback Hill. We could follow, but halfway up the hill they would take flight again. A day could be spent following them from field to field. In the old road field a hare is sitting in the stubble, but when we come to the gate he is off. It is time to go home. The fire is burning well, the breakfast table is laid and the milking long since finished. Step lively, for we must cut down the Wee Field to recover our rabbits. Let the waterhen run for the ditch. She, too, is sacred here.

You have been round with your gun. You have disturbed these quiet hills and fields with your shooting. Come again, was the invitation, and you are welcome. In time it will matter less and less whether you shoot or not. Time will make the carrying of the gun an excuse for hanging about in a hollow, watching the hare, standing on the little hill studying the way a covey moves in a root field. These are the pastures I promised you. The pastures new, like the river, new every time you look at them, never the same two days running, but new forever to those who walk with their eyes open.